REFUGE, RESEARCH AND RELIGION

(A Partial Autobiography)

R B Raikow

This autobiography is "partial" because is deals only with the parts of my life that may be of interest to the general public, and it mostly omits stories of my husband and children that are vital to me personally.

Gotham Books

30 N Gould St.
Ste. 20820, Sheridan, WY 82801
https://gothambooksinc.com/

Phone: 1 (307) 464-7800

© 2024 *R B Raikow*. All rights reserved.

No part of this book may be reproduced, stored in a retrieval system, or transmitted by any means without the written permission of the author.

Published by Gotham Books (August 16, 2024)

ISBN: 979-8-3303-0381-6 (H)
ISBN: 979-8-3303-6003-1 (P)
ISBN: 979-8-3303-6004-8 (E)

Because of the dynamic nature of the Internet, any web addresses or links contained in this book may have changed since publication and may no longer be valid.

The views expressed in this work are solely those of the author and do not necessarily reflect the views of the publisher, and the publisher hereby disclaims any responsibility for them.

Table of Contents

Page

PART I

Why and How I Left My Native Land and Found Refuge in a Yellow House

The nation of Czechoslovakia 1
Some personal history 4
Black Spiders 5
Flags 8
Air Aid Shelter 11
Short Lived Liberation 14
Sokolky Slet 18
How Life for Us in Prague Became Intolerable 20
Treading Water 26
Our First Attempt at Escape 30
Our Successful Escape 34
Limbo 41
DPs 45
Immigrants 53
Our Lives in Our New Country 61

PART II

My Biology Research Career

A Short History of the Science of Genetics 67
How Molecular Biology Came to Dominate Genetics 70
How Genes Control Development 74
My PhD Thesis 78

v

How Ecology Influenced my Research 79

Polytene Chromosomes 80

Possible Further Studies 85

What I Did After my Hawaiian Adventure 86

References and footnotes 87

PART III

My Religion, Blessings and Blunders

My New York Phase 89

California and Bob 91

Pittsburgh PA and My Mother 92

Pope John. XXIII (declared to be saint in 2014) 96

Pope Paul VI 99

Other books by the Author 101

PART I

Why and How I Left My Native Land and Found Refuge in a Yellow House

<u>The nation of Czechoslovakia</u>

The region where I was born is now called Czechia or the Czech Republic, since its peaceful separation from Slovakia in 1993. The Czech language has been spoken there for centuries, but how Slavic people settled there is recorded only in legends. One prominent, relatively-modern phase, includes an account of St. Vaclav (Wenceslaus in German), who in the tenth century was Duke of Bohemia (the Western part of Czechoslovakia). He is the patron saint of the Czech people, and his virtues are lauded as the good King Wenceslaus in a popular (English) Christmas carol.

An equestrian statue of St. Vaclav in Vaclavky Namesti (square) in Prague.

In 1867, the Czech-speaking region was integrated into the Austro-Hungarian Empire, which was a conglomeration of various cultures.

In January 1918 (after World War I) an international meeting was convened at Versailles, just outside Paris, to establish the terms of peace. Thirty nations participated, but the representatives of Great Britain, France, United States and Italy dominated the proceedings. One of their declarations was the establishment of an independent country called Czechoslovakia, to consist of three regions that were occupied by three Slavic groups, closely-related by language: the Czechs, Moravians and Slovaks.

As a native Czech speaker, I can understand spoken Slovak, and Moravian, even though they each sound somewhat different and some of words used in each are unique.

Representatives of each of these groups elected Thomas Garrigue Masaryk to be the first president of Czechoslovakia.

The Garrigue middle name of Thomas Masaryk was actually the maiden name of his American- born wife.

The borders of this newly created nation were drawn on the basis of natural topography, and its constitution was modeled on the one used by the United States.

The constitution drafted for Czechoslovakia was actually better than its model at the time, because it granted women the right to vote.

After two decades of peace, in 1938, another international conference was held at Munich, Germany. This conference was once again dominated by Great Britain, France, US and Italy, but this time it included Germany, represented by Adolf Hitler. Hitler demanded that the western border of Czechoslovakia be moved, so the border area, called Sudetenland, be designated to be part of Germany.

The bilingual population of this region was ethnically about 60% Czech and 40% German. The allies, apparently afraid of triggering another world war, acceded to Hitler. (I think that Mussolini, representing Italy, sided with Hitler for different reasons.)

The "Sudetenland" is a forested, mountainous region, which makes it easily defensible. (I think Hitler's major aim was clearing it of Czech fortifications.) Giving into Hitler on this point was apparently a small matter to the larger nations participating in the Munich conference, for they ignored representatives of Czechoslovakia, who pointed out that the Sudetenland housed significantly more Czechs than Germans. These larger nations, including the US, probably thought that it was not prudent to annoy Hitler over a dispute concerning our tiny country, which was just beginning its independence.

The compromise signed with Hitler at Munich encouraged Hitler's megalomania: The peace we enjoyed after WWI, soon ended and Austria, Poland, and Czechoslovakia fell into Hitler's clutches by 1939.

Some personal history

My father attended Prague's Charles University, where he earned a Doctor of Law degree. He established a successful practice in Prague as a defense lawyer, which enabled him to support his family in middle-class comfort.

His father had been a rector of a private school. He also painted portraits and still life, and earned some money by restoring old oil paintings.

My mother was born in a rural town, just outside of Prague. Her father brought his family to the big city, Prague, to pursue (I think) some white-collar work. I recall him as the kind grandfather, who lived with us in our large Prague apartment.

I never knew either of my grandmothers because they both died before I was born.

I don't know how my parents met, but I think they were drawn together by their shared love of music, especially opera. Mother had a high soprano voice, which she displayed at garden parties before World War II. During those good times, father also took singing lessons and did some stage acting, maybe encouraged by the success of one of his brothers, who was then a prominent opera singer in Prague.

Black Spiders

In March 1939 (the very month of my birth) Goose-stepping Nazis marched into Prague. Soon their black Swastica symbols were all around us like swarming spiders.

It is sad how the Nazis took over and corrupted the Swastica, which was a symbol in ancient India. Ironically it had originally stood for peace.

As a child I saw the black Swastica on insignias of universally hated policemen and on flags, flown everywhere (while display of our Czech flag was forbidden). The image still triggers fear in me. My older sister, Shari, told me how she always recalled the awful sound made by collective Nazi boots as they hit Prague's cobblestoned streets. Nazi atrocities that we heard about during the war, such as the deliberate destruction of a Czech town called, Lidice (described below), left scars on everyone.

During the six years of World War II, most people in Prague did not experience outright physical danger (provided they were not Jewish) because bombs did not fall on us until 1945, but everyone suffered from loss of freedom to speak one's mind and inability to move about. Food shortages were common: the only milk available was diluted (it actually appeared bluish) and eggs were a rarity. Even cans of Ken-L-Ration (horse meat for dogs) were used in some of our dishes. Fresh produce was hard to come by. (One day, my father brought home some bananas. The bananas were way past their prime, with dark peels and a mushy interior. We had to eat them with a spoon.)

Most law offices, including my father's, managed to maintain some business during the war, because the Nazis were sticklers for precision (one good German trait they did not lose). I know that my father saved some people from the concentration camps by providing papers testifying that they had more than fifty percent non-Jewish ancestry. (I think he sometimes used "creative paperwork".)

Our parents tried to make sure that my sister and I received some schooling in the arts. We had piano lessons from a former member of the national symphony, who was desperate for income. He had a nervous tick. Sometimes we attended the opera, which was still occasionally staged because the Nazis looked favorably on a German or Italian repertoire.

Air-raid sirens went off daily. They announced approaching allied planes, but everyone ignored these warnings. We were convinced that the planes were on their way to bomb targets in Germany. Our parents tried to shelter me, but they couldn't keep all of the war away. I remember once seeing a darkly dressed lady sitting at our dining room table. The lady touched my cheek with cold fingers. She wept. Somehow I learned that she was trying to get help for her relatives who were being deported to a concentration camp.

In another incident, the doorbell rang unexpectedly, followed by a loud banging on the door. "Heil Hitler!" barked some men in black, with red arm bands featuring the hated Swastica symbol, as they snapped their stabbing solutes. "We will question everyone in your household!" Mother showed them into the living room. "Look carefully at these uniforms! Have you ever seen these?" Several large, hand colored, photographs were held up, but mother just shook her head. Then the men noticed my eleven-year-old sister, Shari, peeking into the room. "We will question her too," they insisted. Mother protested to no avail.

"I was already shown these in school." Shari tried to tell mother, who hushed her and pulled her close.

The photos were of mannequins dressed in British uniforms. The Gestapo was hunting some soldiers who had managed to assassinate Reinhard Heydrich, the leader of the Nazi SS elite corps in charge of Czechoslovakia. These British-subsidized paratroopers hid themselves in a church basement and shot themselves when they were being discovered by the Nazis.

Then the Nazi's devised a punishment for the entire Czech nation, whom they called "vermin": They randomly picked a town, outside of Prague, called Lidice.

In June, 1942, Lidice was completely destroyed: The adults were shot or sent to concentration camps, where they were gassed; their houses were flattened, and their young children were sent to Germany to be "Aryanized".

Once during that awful time I somehow overheard that there were bad men on the streets with razor blades. This idea grew in my mind. I imagined men dressed in black, sneaking up behind people and swiftly cutting their necks. Then I thought one would feel warm blood streaming around one's neck before feeling pain. I insisted on always wearing a heavy neck scarf. Good thing it was wintertime.

Flags

I often curled up under a large perina (down comforter) on parents' bed in the morning, relishing the moments before I would have to get dressed. One day, in late 1944, as I laid there while mother sat at her dressing table massaging Nivea cream into her face and neck, Ruzena, our maid (who now doubled as a cook) shouted from the balcony where she was airing out pillows: "Pani Boruvkova, you've got to come and see this, I can't believe my eyes!"

Mother, looking puzzled, walked to the balcony. Across the street, a large Czech flag was waving on a pole. Against a gray building, the bright, red, white and blue seemed alive in the morning breeze.

"My God," gasped mother, "Who could be responsible?," and added under her breath: " We may all be punished."

She noticed me standing behind her and tightened her lips. "Why aren't you getting dressed?" I could tell something exciting was up so I quickly complied.

"Isn't that another Czech flag down the street?" Ruzena was leaning over the railing now. "That settles it. I'm going to find out what's going on." She plopped the pills on our unmade bed and rushed out of the room.

Mother dialed the phone. "Hello, this is Pani Bor......, " she started, then stopped.

Apparently the clerk in father's office was connecting her call to father. There was a long pause during which her face alternated from a worried frown to wide astonishment. "But Sharicka (my sister's name in diminutive) has already left," she said at last, and the worried look returned. Finally she nodded, "OK, please hurry." After she hung up, faint pops could be heard outside. Mother closed the balcony door, drew the drapes, and turned on our large wooden radio. As the radio warmed up, the same sounds heard before from outside came out of the radio, loud and clear. Then a breathless voice said: "Freedom is returning. The Czech Nation is reclaiming its place in history." This announcement was followed by the sweet strains of the Czech national anthem. It was familiar to me, but I knew we had been forbidden to sing it. The words celebrate rushing rivers and orchards with blooming trees. Mother's eyes filled with tears.

Ruzena returned with some red, white and blue cotton cloth. "I was lucky to get these" she said as she displayed the folded fabric. "It seems a lot of people are planning to make flags." Father came home from work early and when Shari returned from school parents hugged her as if she had returned from hell. We kept the radio on constantly. The program consisted of the Czech national anthem interspersed with messages like: "Prague is calling all allies! Please come to help liberate us." Every few minutes another voice would come on asking people to help build barricades in the streets.

Father went out for a while, but mother got so upset about it that he didn't do it again. He told us that an old neighbor was out there carrying cobble stones for a barricade. "He had white gloves on and could barely lift them," remarked father as he tried to find news on a short wave radio.

We females kept busy making flags. Shari drew the designs and I colored them. We did not need to make a Czech flag, for mother had saved one hidden in a drawer under the table linen. We were uncertain about the order of the horizontal, red, white and blue stripes on the French tricolor, although everyone agreed that the white stripe should be in the middle. After mother cut out each part, Ruzena worked the old sewing machine. Mother made a cardboard star to help us with the American flag. We traced the cardboard image on white fabric and carefully cut each star out. Mother sewed them on a blue rectangle by hand, not bothering to put them on both sides because we planned to hang the flags down from the balcony railing so only one side would show. Making the American flag was hard, even though we did not try to put the right number of stars and stripes on it, but the British Union Jack was the hardest. Shari tried to draw the design, but it never looked quite right. "It's no use, we have to find a picture somewhere." We had no luck looking through books and so the British flag remained missing in our balcony display. Finally for the Soviet flag mother sacrificed a yellow summer dress, from which she cut out the star, hammer and sickle.

Air Aid Shelter

Mother begged father to stay home, but she need not have bothered because there was no business as usual. The wail of air raid sirens was nothing new. But in the past, these sirens were ignored, because we were convinced that they announced planes on their way to some strategic German targets. Now however, they were suddenly followed by noises like thunder. (I later learned that some allied planes had dropped bombs on us, mistaking Prague for a German city.) One explosion blew out a window in my sister's and my bedroom. Broken glass spilled into the room, covering stuffed animals that I had lined up on a bench. The sound of shattering glass blended with my scream, which was high-pitched and loud, almost like the sirens. Father picked me up, blanket and all, and we all ran down the stairs of our apartment house, which had an underground movie theatre that now served as an air raid shelter. Soon the place was filled. Many people were in bathrobes and had uncombed hair. Even though we, children were kept away in the back, I caught sight of some people being brought in on stretchers. Some had white bandages with red blotches. Ruzena (our maid and cook) refused to come to the shelter. "I will not hide like a rat," she said.

We stayed down there for about three days. It's hard to be sure, since we napped often and there was no daylight. Ruzena brought us whatever food she could find, and although I was usually fond of them I began to get tired of dumplings and sauerkraut. Thankfully there was fresh running water in the theater's rest room. Shari and I were at first excited to explore the empty movie theatre. But soon it was boring to be in the dark, stuffy place. The adults were certainly in no mood for fun. "Couldn't they at least show some movies?", my sister asked once, and was quickly hushed by mother who was constantly straining to listen for explosions.

When the outside remained quiet for a whole day, people started to drift away and father went out to investigate. He came back with a strained smile. "Come on milacci" (darlings), he said, "let's get some fresh air. Ruzena is preparing a real meal for us. She saved a canned ham for the occasion." As mother and my sister got up to follow father, I was gripped with a sense of panic. I remembered mother's anxiety and the blood stains on the white bandages. I pulled on mother's skirt, begging her not to go out. Father picked me up and tried to comfort me. I buried my face into his shoulder. We had to walk up the four flights of stairs to our apartment because we were afraid the elevator might be damaged. There was smoke in the street and a red glow in the sky.

Eventually the smoke faded and new soldiers marched in the street. Their green uniforms seemed more friendly that the Nazi black ones. We hung our homemade flags proudly from our balcony. Mother dressed Shari and me in Czech folk costumes and we waved to the passing soldiers.

Even then the refreshing blue and white of our flags seemed dominated by a sea of red. Still the red Soviet flag with its splash of sunny yellow in the corner seemed to be an improvement over the banners with the awful black swastikas. Most of us were unaware of the new menace starting to infect our land.

Short Lived Liberation

Czech patriots took over the radio and reported news about street fighting against the Nazis, announcing calls for help to aid our liberation. Finally, Russian soldiers marched into Prague. We learned later that British troops, who were present relatively closer to Prague than the Russians, were barred from coming to us because Stalin had convinced the Western Allies that Prague should be liberated by our Slavic brothers.

Eventually, the spider-like swastikas of the Nazi occupiers, were mostly swept away, and our city was filled with Russian soldiers. This seemed then to be a good thing since most Czechs have warm feelings toward Russian culture.

We were still full of hope when father announced: "Let's go to Krkonose for a vacation."

The Krkonose Mountain range is part of the border region that had been given to Hitler at Munich in 1938. But after World War II, it became once again a part of our country. It has always been a favorite area for skiing.

"A great idea," said mother. "We will have to get outfits and skis for all of us." I could see father frowning just slightly. (Finances were tight.)

The Krkonose, snow-covered hills, dotted with evergreen trees, were just the thing for blotting out our memories of war-broken bodies and buildings. I slid happily down slopes on small skis, not even needing poles for balance.

After we returned to the city, mother gave a party for father's fiftieth birthday. Of course this party was something for grownups, but I couldn't help sneaking a peek into the brightly lit living room filled with guests. I overheard conversations that made little sense to me: "How can you call it an election with only one slate on the ballot? Many will be afraid to use the 'no' ballot because we have to hand in the unused one."

For this "election" people were given two cards one for yes and one for no to the proposed Communist takeover. They were required to place one into a ballot box and hand the unused card to an attendant. People were afraid of being "registered" as an opposer to the Commies.

One man stood up to get a refill of wine, and exclaimed. "Who cares how one votes anyway? They'll call the result whatever they want."

The coming election was also a subject at my school: A hefty woman in a beige suit, with yellowish hair in a bun, came to our school. A gleaming medal with a red star on her lapel was her only decoration. "Do you know, children, about the voting that your parents will soon participate in?" We all sat in silence. Something about her broad smile made me wary. "Why do you think some people want to go behind a curtain to cast their ballots?" she continued in a commanding voice. No one offered an answer. Even at age of seven, I sensed that any real discussion was not welcome. "Well," the visitor continued standing straighter, "I always cast my vote before the curtain because I am proud to be part of the movement to make a great new society where everyone will be equal and everyone will be happy." She was beaming and some of the children started smiling with her.

But not me. All I knew was that my friend and nanny, Emila, was gone. (You see her family was German, and there were some ugly reprisals in Prague against innocent people who had a German background. Some Germans were even hung from lamp posts. Father, feared for her safety, and advised her to go back home.)

In an attempt to voice opposition and still be able to hand in the "no" card to the authorities, the underground distributed photographs of Jan Masaryk, who was the politically active son of our beloved first president, Thomas Masaryk. These photographs were the same size and shape as the official ballots so they could be placed into the voting boxes without arousing suspicion. Many had hopes that Jan Masaryk would lead an opposition to the Communists.

The "election" of 1946 was declared, as expected, to be a Communist landslide.

In 1948 Jan Masaryk was found dead, beneath his upstairs window. The newspapers stated that he had committed suicide. (Most people suspected that he was pushed.) A few month later, Eduard Benes, who had been our second, duly elected president, and who presided over a Czech government in exile during the war, was dead at age sixty four. His body was laid out in state, and long lines of people filed past his coffin to pay their respects. Some thought that strategic flowers were placed around his body to hide a bullet wound.

At that time I had a friend named Ludka, and we sometimes played unsupervised in a park before a nearby church. (This unusual freedom was allowed me because mother now had to cook, clean and scrape up the ingredients for our meals without any help. Even if we could have afforded a maid, the new regime did to allow anyone to do such "servile" labor for the "corrupt bourgeoisie".) Ludka and I made shallow indentations with our heels in the ground, and putted clay marbles. In the shadows of the flying buttresses of the Gothic St.Ludmila's Church, we found some multicolored glass fragments. They were remnants of the stained glass windows, shattered during the bombing at the end of the war.

One day a bandstand was set up in the square before the church, and placards advertised that children, freed from Nazi concentration camps, were to be honored. The small victims marched obediently onto the stage. They were emaciated with sparse, rust-colored hair, but the most horrible sights were some scars, which were ceremonially displayed. Somehow I understood that these poor, little children, had been the subjects of experiments in the concentration camps to determine the effect of age on the rate of wound healing.

Sokolky Slet

I fondly recall another event, which happened at that time: the Sokol Slet (convocation) held in Prague in 1948. Sokol is a unique, group exercise program, founded in Prague in 1867. No one in my immediate family was particularly athletic, but in 1948 we all participated. This non-political activity was felt by everyone to be a way of asserting our Czech identity. Ordinary people of all ages met each week to practice for that upcoming, national event. Instructions for the exercises, to be held on a huge outdoor field, were sent to local Sokol chapters all over the country. The maneuvers were devised by choreographers to be performed to original music.

Each age group had their uniforms. I, along with thousands of grammar school aged girls, dressed in a short bright red skirt attached to a top in beige cotton, trimmed with red. Shari's outfit was a short blue gym-suit complemented by a white, plastic, hand-held ring. Mother's uniform was a dark blue skirt and a white peasant blouse and father exercised in dark blue, stretch trousers and a white sleeveless tee shirt.

The position where each person was to stand in a huge field was indicated on a grid, laid out on the ground. Loud speakers built into the ground announced each move, and monitors, overlooking the whole from above, alerted anyone on the field who stepped out of line.

Remarkably all came off without any obvious hitches. Imagine a huge field suddenly turning from white to navy as thousands of perfectly lined up adults bent over, or a bright blue field of teenagers erupting with a cloud of white as they lifted their plastic rings into the air. My group did circle dances, accompanied by sung poems, set to music.

It may seem strange to someone who wasn't there, but the sheer spectacle of thousands of people doing the same motion in perfect synchrony was breathtaking. The show lasted several days before large audiences. Everyone loved it, spectators and participants alike. (There may have been more participants, in one event or another, than pure spectators.)

Shortly after the various participants returned to their homes all over the county, the Communist authorities outlawed Sokol. This was the final straw that convinced all of us that the new regime was evil. Why did they squelch this wholesome activity? Many showed their opposition to the new regime by wearing a homemade pin: a small nail entwined with string. These represented the names of two well known, and soon arrested dissidents, Hrebik and Provazova. (Their names mean nail and string in the Czech language.)

How Life for Us in Prague Became Intolerable

For a while, my family remained relatively well-off because father's law practice continued. However, we were classified as "corrupt bourgeoisie", so our imminent downfall became inevitable. Then our lives abruptly shifted:

The following section, describing my father's arrest, was written by my sister, who was thirteen years old when we lived this.

I woke up suddenly that night in 1948. There was a vague sensation of something unusual in the air. In a child's bed with high sides, my sister was breathing regularly. I sat up, only half conscious, and noticed that the bed of the woman by the window was empty. I didn't like this woman. It was uncomfortable to have a strange person in my room, especially one that persisted saying that spoiled daughters of rich parents should be spanked and not allowed to do whatever they want.

Yesterday the woman was baking a cake and whipped egg whites and yolks together at one time. Having seen mother and the cook bake such cakes before, I said, quite innocently: "You're doing it all wrong. That cake will be hard and dry, and fall to the bottom of the pan." (Well, maybe it really wasn't innocent. I did say it on purpose to belittle her.) The woman became terribly aggravated and proceeded to bake the cake her own way. Of course, it ended up flat and hard.

Then she complained loudly to mother: "I simply won't have a child tell me how to manage my profession," she whimpered. All the while the woman clutched a handkerchief and kept touching the tip of her nose with it. I couldn't help noticing that the hanky was dirty and that it had a monogram of mother's initials: 'PB'. It was awful to see the woman blow her nose into a handkerchief that I myself might later use. Why do we have disgusting people living here?

The day a new woman came into our apartment, I heard mother say: "Now I'll have someone to keep me company in my hard days." What hard days? Father now didn't have to do much traveling. (This was actually because he had less business out of town.) Things seemed almost the same as they used to be.

There was a soft noise by the bedroom door, but I couldn't see the door. (There was a little alcove to the right of my bed and the door was at the end of it.) Then I heard a thud and a groan. Clearly the woman was now by the door. I became more curious than sleepy. Leaning over the edge of my bed I could see the end of the alcove. The woman was sitting on the floor. Her head was pressed against the curtained, glass door. Her large, bare feet trembled with cold and she kept trying to wrap them up in the blanket she had thrown over her shoulders. "What's the matter?" I whispered, embarrassed at the woman's behavior.

"Shhhh!" She waved her hand to push me away, but then continued almost soundlessly: "They came about an hour ago. Your mother didn't call me, but I want to know what's going on."

"Let me hear too!"

"All right, but don't make any noise. Your mother would tell me off if she found out I let you stand on this cold floor barefooted."

I crouched next to the woman. "Why are they here?"

The woman leaned toward a beam of light escaping from underneath the curtains. "Oh, Jesus, Mary and Joseph! I knew this peace wouldn't last." She started to talk quickly. "Three of them, in big, thick, fur coats, sitting in the dining room, and it's almost one o'clock in the morning. They want the Doctor."

"Daddy?" The woman didn't answer this time. Curiosity got the better of her and she carefully opened the door. I looked out eagerly. The light blazed full in the dining room across the hall and I heard mother's voice, high-pitched, intermixed with suppressed sobs. I watched and listened, closing my eyes occasionally to hear better. The men sat around our large table. One of them stretched his legs. Another was moving his foot over the nap of the brown rug. They didn't seem exactly comfortable, but their faces wore expressions of routine. They glanced now and then at mother, who sat shivering before them. She had stopped her continuous flow of words, and with a twitching hand seemed to be painstakingly scratching lines into the glistening table surface. Then she bent her head back and sighed heavily, not just once, but continuously breathing sighs, as a person that has no more tears.

"Please, listen to me," she started again. This time she spoke with desperation. "Please, you are men of experience. Policemen deal with all sorts, but you can believe me.." She rubbed her eyes.."My husband is a very good man. What are they accusing him of? He was one of the greatest anti-Nazi workers during the war. In this very room where you are sitting, we kept escaped camp prisoners at our expense. My husband is a patriot. This is all nonsense. How can they build any sort of charge. Is it wrong to have money when you made it with your own head or hands?"

Finally one of the men spoke as if trying to spare himself the flood of emotion thrown at him by mother. "Lady, don't tell this to us. We have orders to take your husband in and that's it."

"Animals! That's all you are. You come to drag a man out of his peaceful bed, in the middle of the night. " Mother had finally lost it.

"But Pani Boruvkova, your husband isn't home. Wherever he is, we have orders to take him in and are prepared to wait for him as long as it takes."

Mother closed her eyes. "He will come soon," she whispered as if to herself. "Tuesdays he spends the evening at the men's club. He always comes home late."

"We'll wait," both repeated monotonously.

A key sounded in the doorway...

When the door closed behind the four men, the woman, up to now silently listening on the floor next to me, got up, and walked toward mother who remained motionless in the dining room. I started up too, suddenly drawn with inexpressible emotion. "Mummy!" I cried as I clutched her. Then mother walked slowly to the bedroom with movements of a person bereft of all hope.

I am now continuing Shari's story with my own account.

Father did not come home for many days. Mother didn't explain it, at least not to me. For a while, I thought that father was on one of his business trips, but soon I could tell something bad was happening: Mother let us sleep with her in the big bed in the master bedroom. I had always wanted to do so in the past, but now it seemed it was mother who needed comforting.

Some of it started to get clearer on the day when mother took us to visit father. She told us that father wanted to see our report cards and we rode the streetcar to a big drab looking building. Mother was visibly nervous. We sat in a room that was bare except for a long table and some benches. Suddenly the door opened and father came in. He looked thin and tired.

"Hello little ones," he said smiling broadly, and hugged us. I remained stiff. (Hugs were not a usual greeting in our family.) Mother looked on, stifling tears. Then she took our report cards from her purse and handed them to father. "I am very proud of both of you," father said looking them over. Mother handed him a pen and he signed them. I simply don't remember what else was done or said. My mind was kind of numbed by it all.

I do not fully understand why mother took us there. Perhaps she felt it was necessary to pretend to us and to the school authorities that father was still living with us. But now I also wonder whether mother had some inkling that we might lose father somehow soon. Much later I learned that father was being detained in prison for questioning. The Communists kept people locked up like that indefinitely, in Pangrac Jail.

Father recorded what happened to him during and after his prolonged interrogation in a letter to mother, which I found later. In it he described how, after they released him, he had to sneak out of the country to avoid what could have been his death by hanging. The Pangrac Jail building (shown below) was site of executions during the Nazi and Communist eras.

Here are some examples of what father endured in jail. (I'm not exactly sure of how I learned of these. It may have been from father's diary, or from overheard discussions.)

Father shared a cell with some other men, whom the Communists called "bourgeois pigs", but who were just relatively wealthy owners of businesses. Their cell had only metal cots with thin, bare mattresses. A toilet with no seat in one corner was the only other furnishing. The men became good friends, sharing their meals, which were mostly provided by my mother and the other mens' wives. (The jail encouraged this so-called "home maintenance" to save money.) The jailed men were deliberately given no water. They were told: "There's water in the toilet!". Instinct for survival forced them to devise a schedule: The toilet was allowed to be used for its intended purpose only during the night and in the morning. The whole day it was flushed several times, and wiped out thoroughly with rags. In the evening all drank from it using their cupped hands.

Mother tried everything to get father released. She even managed to see the wife of our former, beloved president, Eduard Benes. But all was to no avail. Many days passed and I imagine my father, in the Pangrac Jail, was beginning to lose his grip on reality, when an official at the court, who knew father because of his previous function as lawyer, told father that his family was coming to visit, gave him a change of clothes and arranged for him to take a shower. (Maybe as father stepped into that shower he thought about the Nazi "showers" in concentration camps, where lethal gas was fed in instead of water. Everyone knew the jails could hold no more.) Still, father managed to put on his old relaxed smiling face as he approached mother, Shari and me, on that report card signing day.

Years later, after we were settled in the US, I remember that I stupidly made my father angry by implying that he must have been involved with something shady to have been detained in jail for so long. Father was so hurt that he spent several evenings writing out the story of why he was arrested: He was accused of collaborating with the Nazis - a charge without a hint of truth. Cleary he was a political prisoner: Being a lawyer, who fought for people's property rights, did not sit well with the Communist hacks in charge.

Treading Water

As detailed in his writing, father was eventually released from jail (without any charges), but his friends at the jail, whom he knew from his years as a defense lawyer, advised him to leave the country immediately. "The Communist authorities are not done with you," they warned him. So father snuck out of Czechoslovakia into Germany.

He managed (I don't know how) to inform mother about his immigration via a short note which in essence said: "Some former colleagues, still working at the jail, told me that my file was on the director's desk, and the rumor was that I must hang! I am now safe and will arrange our reunion soon."

During this time mother managed to keep us living in relative normalcy.

One day she set out our fancy dinner dishes on our bare dining room table. Seeing them brought back memories of our festive Christmas dinners, when the dishes were filled with delicious food. She ran her fingers over the fluted edges of a serving bowl, when the doorbell rang. Noticing me watching her, she squared her shoulders. "That must be the antiques dealer I am expecting. Would you answer the door for me, dear?" she said as she blew her nose.

At the door were two young men whom I recognized as regulars frequenting the party headquarters located on the first floor of our apartment building. "We have come to remove your telephone," one said arrogantly. "The people need your telephone!" the other explained. Mother was behind me now, and, to my surprise, she seemed to stifle a laugh. The two hesitated a bit, apparently taken aback by her cheerfulness, but then they grew bolder, as if they saw her attitude evidence for the justice of their cause.

After they disconnected our phone and left without a word, I said reproachingly: "Mother, how can you be so cheerful? We now have no phone!"

"Forgive me Dadlicku," (that's a diminutive of the name, Dadla, which was my nickname for some reason) "those two struck me as schoolboy bullies. It's better to keep a sense of humor." She squeezed my hand." We'll be alright. Hopefully we'll not have to stay here much longer."

Mother was incredibly strong in those days. I didn't know it then, but a lot of her strength came from the notes she regularly received from father. The letters were always hand-delivered by the same man. Father never signed them. Instead he used a code name: "Sylvia". This code name had been established in the first note: After assuring mother that he was OK, he said that he would always sign his letters with the name of one of our cats, "the one who loved your singing so." Mother was a trained singer and in the old days she used to sing at social gatherings. That cat, Sylvia, would always come running when she heard her singing. (All this information about these letters wasn't shared with me until much later. I guess at age nine I could not be completely trusted to keep a secret.)

I also learned later that mother was followed for many days after father had left. Apparently the police thought that she might give away father's whereabouts, since they were unable to shake her resolve at their headquarters. She told us (after we were all safe, of course) that she even reproached the Commies at their headquarters for not being able to locate her husband, who she claimed had left her. She also told us that she would sometime turn and smile at a man tailing her, and tell him: "Why don't you grab a cup of coffee while I go in here to take care of something."

It seems incredible to me that the Commies took so much trouble about our family. As far as I know, father was not in any way involved with politics. He only had some clients that were fighting property confiscations.

A Polish lady came occasionally to help mother during this time. When their chores were finished, mother and this lady would sit at our dining room table while the lady told mother her fortune with cards. "All will turn out well," she'd say, and mother would dab her eyes. "I see you settled in a far off land, and there you will have a third daughter."

"What? Wait, that's going too far!" mother said then.

Mother recalled this years later when Andrea, my sister's baby daughter came to live with us in Brooklyn. Then mother said then: "See the prophesy came true."

Sometimes that lady told mother about things she had witnessed in Poland. Her Czech was intermixed with Polish, but this didn't bother mother, who prided herself on understanding several Slavic languages. I remember that Polish lady saying that she saw a big pile covered with some sort of canvas. She said, "I noticed that it was moving! "Hoopalo to hoopalo!" (Polish for, "Moved it moved, it moved!!"). (I don't know how I understood that the sheet was covering a pile of bodies and that some of the people under the canvass may have been partly alive!)

My sister, Shari, always talented in music and art, was a teenager by then. Mother couldn't afford to pay to continue our piano lessons but Shari's slender hands continued daily piano practice. The teachers at school, all solid Communist party members, sometimes forced Shari to go on work brigades, e.g. to pick potatoes. "Just look at my hands," she would say as she showed us her hands with ground in dirt. Mother tried convincing her to see it as an opportunity for healthy exercise and fresh air, but I could see that she felt sorry for her.

Despite those hard times, mother would not let my sister's adolescence go by without some structured socializing. So, as was the traditional for teenagers her age, she arranged for her to go to ballroom dancing where young people practiced poise. My sister then had a boyfriend, a pre-med student. (I'm not sure how they met.) He seemed to me the ultimate in sophistication. I imagine she was the envy of her contemporaries at the dancing classes because of him. I, alas, was too young for such things. Getting ready for the dancing class was usually a big production: "I can't go with this puffy face," Shari would sob after another crying scene about her dress. Mother eventually always fixed her face with a bit of makeup. Seeing the makeup ritual, I decided to try it myself:

"Such pretty rosy cheeks on my little girl" mother remarked to me one day. So from that day on I would often color my cheeks with rouge. I wanted to make mother smile for a change.

I was kept in the dark about what we heard from father, to ensure I wouldn't tell anyone, but I learned about this later, so I will relate the following here in context:

Periodically the same man, a Mr Vanya, would bring notes to mother from father. Mr Vanya rarely spoke and always left immediately after handing mother an envelope. Mother prudently destroyed each note after she read it. Father kept assuring her that he was alright and eventually that he had managed to find a job, but he never spelled out any details that could give away where he was. In one note there were instructions for us to file for passports so we could visit some distant relatives in Paris. Mother tried, but the passports were never granted.

Our First Attempt at Escape

Then one of father's notes read: "Take the 6 PM train to Klatovy on March 4. Carry only small pieces of baggage that you can easily handle yourselves. At the Klatovy railroad station a man wearing a marigold in his lapel will meet you and give you further instructions."

Klatovy is a town near the border between Czechoslovakia and Germany. We had visited there previously because in this town there is a monument in honor of our paternal great, great grandfather, Jan Krejci, a famous geologist, who was born there. Here is a photo of this monument. The rocks at the bottom are probably examples of minerals he had studied.

Nothing was explained to me, but I knew that something big was up.

"We are going on a trip," mother said to me. "We may not be back for a long time. You can take with you whatever can fit in this bag." Then she handed me a small satchel.

"I must take my doll babies" I said. "I can't leave them here to fend for themselves." So I packed two dolls. Mother added some underwear, lifted the bag and approved its weight.

Shari seemed to have a clear understanding that we might not return. "Oh I don't care to take anything. I am already leaving my heart behind," she sobbed.

Mother packed the most useful clothes she could find. Where she could, she stuffed our birth certificates, her marriage certificate, and a few family photographs. She picked out the most comfortable shoes and clothes for us to wear.

Before we sat down for a light supper, we walked through the entire apartment. Mother scanned the books and paintings in the living room. She closed the lid of the piano in the corner of the dining room and then went into the entrance room decorated in oriental style. She opened the closet that lined the wall and fingered father's suits. Finally we all laid down on the white carved bed in parents' bedroom and mother covered her eyes with her arm.

We were awakened by our grandfather. He had tears in his eyes. (Mother had made arrangements for her father to go live with her sister, Marie. Up until then, this maternal grandfather had been living with us.) I just sat wide-eyed on the big bed in our parents' room not understanding why he was so upset. He gave Shari and me hugs.

Then we splurged on the luxury of a taxi to the railroad. My sister's boyfriend traveled with us on the train to the outskirts of the city. Shari and he stood with their arms around each other on the back platform. "Heavens what a fuss, these young people make," mother said to some embarrassed ladies looking at the couple. "They will be separated for a while. You'd think it was the end of the world."

We found the small Klatovy station deserted. There was no man with a marigold. We waited on the platform for what seemed to me a long time. Finally, we went to a small boarding house near the station. "It won't do to just turn around and go home," mother said. "We must stay for few days to make it believable that we came here for a vacation."

The next morning, Shari spotted a sign in a shop across the street. It said, "REAL WHIPPED CREAM FOR SALE TODAY." She said that she remembered whipped cream, but I had never tasted it. So we dived into the shop with mother's blessing. The alleged whipped cream was served in small glass bowls with a few wild strawberries. "This isn't like I remember," Shari remarked.

"Well it seems appropriate that this is sour cream. Nothing is right in this country anymore," sighed mother. We ate it all anyway.

After two days of hiking in the woods, we returned to Prague. When we stepped into our apartment we got a shock: It seemed that everything movable was gone. Mother went to a corner phone booth to call her sister. It turned out that our relatives had taken whatever they could move, carrying out the things as best they could, even using our old baby carriage. They said they didn't want to leave anything for the Reds. We managed to get back a few dishes and some bedding.

In the morning, mother and I were looking over the pantry next to the front door, which miraculously still contained a couple of cans of food. Suddenly there were loud bangs on the door. Mother opened the door, just as the superintendent of our apartment, was about to unlock it. He and some official looked startled to see us. "What's the meaning of this?" mother said indignantly.

"Pardon us, pani, but we were under the impression that your family had vacated" they said timidly and slinked away.

"Maybe this aborted attempt at escape was a good thing," mother said later as we laid on the big bed "They might think twice about jumping to conclusions next time."

Our Successful Escape

After we settled into our ransacked apartment, I could see that mother was trying very hard not to lose her grip. She kept saying, not to worry, that father would come through for us. She might have been even more worried had she known what father was going through then. We learned about this later.

Father was living on the outskirts of Frankfurt in Germany. He was employed as a writer for a Czech-language newspaper, New Yorksy Listy, which was published in New York City. The European staff of this newspaper consisted mostly of former political prisoners from Czechoslovakia. Each day Father learned how much harder things were getting back in Czechoslovakia from his coworkers, who had contacts with the Czech underground. He kept trying, with their help, to arrange our escape.

I am here imagining what took place in their office on a day after the Klatovy escape failure:

"It was really bad!" Someone said just as father walked into their office. All of them looked at father with pained expressions, because they knew that we had been scheduled to take that route.

"What are you talking about!" Father said, looking around.

"You might as well know," said the head of the office, "Klatovy," (Father's throat tightened.)" is, well, a goner. We lost all those guides….one person shot - others arrested!"

"Any news of my family?" He almost shouted.

"We think your family was not involved at all… Their contact was arrested before your family could meet him…"

Then father sought out the one man he felt might be able to help, his most reliable friend in the underground, Mr Vanya. He was the man who so faithfully delivered letters to mother, being able somehow to move back and forth easily across the border.

When I wrote this in 2014, the only person left in our family that was part of this was my sister, Shari. When she read this part of my account she said I had some of the details wrong: She thought that our escape was arranged by someone from the "Central Intelligence Core" because father was acquainted with them. Shari did not remember a Mr. Vanya. (But I clearly remember mother speaking of him, and that it was he who delivered father's letters.) Shari thought that the letters were delivered by someone who was a conductor on President Benes' train, which was sort of a 1940's equivalent of the American Air force One. For all I know this conductor <u>was</u> Mr. Vanya. Anyway I am leaving the story the way I originally wrote it because it conveys the emotions we all felt.

"OK", said Mr. Vanya, after father inquired about arranging our escape. "It can be done, but it will cost a lot of money. Not for me, you know that, but we have to pay the border guards and some local farmers. I trust them, but I can't ask them to risk their lives without a substantial material reward." Father did all he could. He sold his gold watch. (The one valuable thing he still owned.) But that, pooled with the money he had managed to save from his small salary, was not enough. Finally a plan was devised: Another family was to go with us. This family had wealthy contacts in Switzerland, which made the financing possible. "I will personally pick up your wife and daughters and drive them to a farmer contact. Don't worry, the plan is almost foolproof," Mr. Vanya tried to reassure father.

Two days after our return from that aborted attempt at escape in Klatovy, just as mother was beginning to despair about how she was going to scrape up enough money to buy food, our doorbell rang early in the morning. She was surprised to see Mr. Vanya, for he had never before come at this time of the day. "Is Sylvia in?" he inquired using the code word. Mother stared at him frozen. "May I come in?" Mother opened the door wider and beckoned him into the dining room.

"Has something happened to my husband?"

"No, all is well with him. Here is his letter. Please don't take the time to read it now," he said as she started to open the envelope. "I have very little time. Your husband has arranged for you to leave with me. Can you be ready tonight?" Mother's shoulders relaxed a bit. It was a relief to have things move so swiftly.

"Yes," Mother said simply.

"Good. I will pick up you and your daughters tonight by car in the back of your apartment house at midnight sharp. I will be driving a black Skoda. Stand in the vestibule, in the back of the building, and come out only after you see me get out of the car and open up the trunk and all the doors of the car." Mother took a breath ready to ask some question, but he put up his hand. "Please forgive me Pani Boruvkova, I have other business to arrange." Then he bowed and left.

In father's hand-writing the letter read:

> *Dear Sylvia, The man who delivers this letter is very experienced. Trust him.*
>
> *I will see you soon.*

Mother turned the letter over, not believing how short it was, then she called to us. "We have to hurry and get ready to leave again." Then she disposed of the letter by burning it in a metal waste can, as had been her habit.

We didn't have to do much since we were still in traveling mode from our trip to Klatovy, so to calm ourselves, we decided to pass the day outside. It was a lovely spring day and we wanted to take a last look at our beloved Prague. From a hill in Petrin Gardens, we looked wistfully over Prague's red-orange roofs and church spires, admiring the cherry trees dotting the hillside and wondered if we would ever see them again, festooned in their pink glory.

We cut short our reverie and made up our minds to concentrate on staying alert. Even I sensed that our lives depended on that. Mother made us take a nap after supper, much to our objections. We dressed for the journey. I looked forward to the adventure ahead.

At a little before midnight, we put on our raincoats and boots, locked up the apartment and rode the elevator to the ground floor. No one was in sight. Our steps echoed as we walked down a long vestibule. The black Skoda pulled up promptly and Mr. Vanya stepped out opening the doors and trunk as predicted. He moved swiftly, motioned us into the car and placed our bags into the trunk. Despite our excitement the three-hour ride made me fall asleep in the back seat. We arrived at a small farm before daybreak. The car was hidden in a barn. My sister and I were made comfortable on some cots. I looked sleepily at the adults sitting around a kitchen table. The other family joining us, was already present. It consisted of an older gentleman, a husband and wife and their teenaged daughter.

"You would all be wise to take a nap," said one of the two guides to whom they were introduced. "We won't start until ten tonight."

Mother, addressed the guide, "I don't know if I will get the opportunity later so I want to thank you for helping us!" He just waved his hand.

"Tell me," jumped in the father of the other family, "what makes you do this kind of work?"

The guide's eyes narrowed. He took a sip of coffee and said. "I'm tired of bullies running our lives. My immediate family was spared being killed by the Nazis, but the trauma they put us through and the loss of our normal way of life will never be made up. Of course all that pales into insignificance in the view of the suffering of my uncle and aunt, who did go to the concentration camps." His voice trailed off and he closed his eyes.

Mother said leaning closer to him: "That era is over now."

"Is it?" he said with sudden force. "Just the other day two of my friends were caught and shot. They had been smuggling medicine to a dear man who couldn't obtain it because of the damned system the Communists have created. They were shot for trying to help a man survive! Idiots for the most part are in charge! They feel insecure, and need to wield their newfound power. I could tick off other examples of their insane so-called justice. We can't fight them openly, but I won't just stand by and do nothing." After this I must have drifted off to sleep because I don't remember anything else.

It was really dark when I was awakened, but it didn't take me long to become alert. We were given home-made bread, bacon and tea. Seven people piled into a car: the two guides and the grandfather of the other family sat in the front. The parents of the other family and us three piled into the back. I sat on my other's lap and the two teenaged girls sat on the floor.

Luckily the ride was only about ten minutes. The car moved without lights. I can still hear the sound of the wheels as it moved slowly on a gravel road. We stopped by a dark forest, and piled out of the car into the sweet smelling night air. We had been instructed to be very quiet and to follow the guides in a single file: The two teenagers, the father of the other family and I pulled up ahead with the younger guide. Mother, the other mother and the older man followed behind us with the other guide. We entered a pine forest. The walk through the forest was easy, for fallen needles formed a soft carpet that prevented most underbrush from growing. "Do you see those lights on the horizon?" whispered our guide as we emerged into a meadow and were told to sit and rest. "They are Selb in Germany. Just keep walking in their direction, and you can't go wrong." I watched the young guide as he started showing off his gun to the two young girls.

Then we walked through some potato fields. The plowed rows were easy for my small feet to navigate, but I could see the adults had trouble finding their footing. I was grateful for the knee high boots mother had bought for us, for here and there I stepped into mud. As the night wore on, I kept my eyes on the row of twinkling lights at the horizon. They seemed to be not very far away at first, but even after a long time of brisk walking, they didn't seem to be getting closer. I started to feel dazed and had to force myself to concentrate on following the dark figure of the guide ahead of me.

We learned later that mother, who was walking further back had a harder time: The old man from the other family started to pant, sat down and asked to be left behind! Mother would have none of it and pulled him along. It must have been hard for her saving this grandfather after she had just left her own father behind.

My sister told me about another incident: She and the young guide were the first to reach a small river. The guide said, "In case they start shooting, just jump into the river. The river is already in Germany." (Shari thought then that water wouldn't really protect her from bullets!) They were walking on a graveled path that paralleled the river, when she stumbled and dropped the satchel she was carrying, it slid down a small hill. Suddenly a voice came out of the bushes. "If you make any more noise, I will have to shoot!" It was a guard who had been generously bribed.

Eventually we crossed a small wooden bridge and came to a pile of logs at the side of the road. "You are in Germany now! Sit here and wait for the others." The young guide, whose name was never mentioned, smiled and ran back down the road.

Mother and the others arrived shortly after that. Their guide also bid us farewell and instructed all of us to wait for an American jeep. "They patrol this road constantly," he said and disappeared into the darkness. As expected an open army jeep came by a few minutes later. It was driven by two uniformed men, members of an American government organization patrolling the borders along the Iron Curtain. Their American English sounded strangely nasal. We were grateful that the parents of the other family spoke English. We managed to squeeze into the jeep, which drove us in a few minutes to a small farmhouse that had been converted to a local headquarters. Shari and I collapsed on some army cots. I couldn't stay awake long, but before I closed my eyes, I saw mother looking out of the window anxiously awaiting father, who was due any minute. I understand that when he did arrive, they drank champagne and went out to look back into the country we had just left.

Limbo

The next day, only half rested but exuberant to be reunited with father, we went by train to a suburb of Frankfurt where father had rented the upstairs of a small house. We ate German sausages at a busy railway station and fell into bed as soon as we arrived. I didn't even complain about the fact that I had to share a bed with my sister. The beds were wonderfully soft with thick feather comforters and pillows.

After about fifteen hours of sleep I was ready to explore our new world. Father had arranged a few days off from work to give us a tour. First he took us to an outdoor market. There, piles of various fresh fruits and vegetables delighted mother. We bought some oranges (fruits that I had never seen before), and bananas that bore little resemblance to the brown ones I had during the war. Then we had lunch at a big cafeteria to which only people employed by American companies were admitted. Father had the proper credentials since he was employed by an American newspaper. "Now I want you to try a real American treat," father said as we gulped down our hamburgers.

"Please tell me it isn't Coca Cola" grimaced my sister. (She had been given a Coke by one of the men at the farm station after our escape and didn't like the strange new taste.)

"Just wait," father smiled as he ordered three vanilla milk shakes. It was like nothing we had ever tasted before, wonderful bubbles enhancing the sweet taste of the rich ice cream. *A great invention, the Americans have here,* I thought.

For weeks we always ate lunch at this American commissary. What impressed mother most, in that large dining area, was the fluffy pastel dresses on some American babies. Military wives with their children were abundant in there, and they spent a great deal of time chatting and smiling at each other. The words "bye bye" were the first I learned in American. It amused my parents when I imitated the American ladies at home, waving goodbye and saying the words with their intonation. I was aware that we looked odd and different in that crowd. We were an obviously European family because of our mannerisms and dress. We had no money for hairdressers, and mother's once shiny hair hung limp and shapeless.

"We'll go to the PX and see what we can buy" said father when mother mentioned how prettily she thought the American children were dressed. It made me dizzy to survey the long shelves lined with different goods. Father picked up some nylons and lacy underwear for the proprietress of the house where we were staying. "If I didn't know better, I might be shocked by your choice of gifts for that woman," mother said with uncharacteristic sarcasm.

Father said a bit sheepishly: "Please believe me that I buy these things because they are what she wants and they are totally unavailable in German stores. She gives us a very good price on the rooms we rent. If it weren't for that and the cheap food we can get because of my access to American facilities, I don't know how we could manage on the small salary I make."

Mother spotted a ream of pink and white cotton that made her visualize her daughters in matching summer dresses. It wasn't easy for her to make the dresses, even with the aid of an old fashioned sewing machine that the landlady lent her. (In the past our clothes were all made by a seamstress.) Eventually the dresses were finished. I was delighted by mine, but it was apparent that my teenage sister would have wished for something less girlish and certainly not something matching little me. Still she didn't say a word. We all witnessed how hard mother had worked.

The days wore on into autumn. Father went daily to the newspaper office and we just maintained order and traveled for our meals in the American cafeteria. Parents did not try enrolling us girls in school because they thought we would be moving within a few months, so Shari and I were becoming colossally bored. The highlight of my sister's week was a Saturday night Bingo held in the PX cafeteria, and she looked forward to the Southern fried chicken, for which she acquired a real liking. Between that and the milkshakes, the once lanky teenager was getting a bit plump. I eventually made friends with two German girls who lived next door. The language barrier between us wasn't much of a problem. "Kook mal", I'd say as I made some new fancy maneuver bouncing a rubber ball off a wall. Our living quarters were extremely small, and the bathing routine was a trial: There was always just enough hot water for only one tub-full, so we took turns on who was to bathe first. My sister and I found it was easier to share the one bed available to us by lying anti-parallel, but I often complained that her big feet were sticking in my face.

Even though we spent little money and bought all necessary consumables taking advantage of the low prices at the PX, father constantly had to draw on his savings and they were now nearly gone. It was late 1949 and the terrible toll of the war was still very evident. People missing arms, legs or eyes were everywhere and about half of Frankfurt's buildings were in ruins. The situation was not much better in Paris, where father tried (to no avail) to find employment with the help of some distant relatives.

"I have come to the conclusion," father said one evening "that we have no choice but to emigrate out of Europe."

"Heavens where could we go?" asked mother, half shocked but also somewhat interested in the prospect.

"Well, we are fortunate because we qualify for Communist refugee status. After we get classified as such, we will have our travel expenses covered by the country to which we choose to emigrate. Apparently the Allies, and especially the United States, are very interested in halting the spread of Communism, and publicizing the plight of people like us helps give Communism a bad name."

"And a well-deserved bad name it is. Just look what they have reduced us to. You have always worked hard. You don't deserve to have to start all over again," said mother.

"What I have started is the paper work for us to be officially declared Communist refugees," continued father, ignoring her remark. "I see no problem so far, and the people at the paper assure me that it shouldn't take long. What we have to do now is decide to what country we wish to go."

"This is interesting. Let's see, I want a nice warm climate, but not someplace where there is no music or theater," said mother dreamily.

"I'm afraid the choice is rather limited. There are only three countries accepting immigrant refugees from Communism at this time. They are Australia, Argentina and the United States."

"Good God- they are all on the other side of the world," gasped mother.

"Well I think, there is no contest. The best choice is the United States because the Americans have the most sound economy now." Nothing more was said. We knew that father was right. Father then officially filed for admission to the U.S. as a Communist refugee family. Upon the advice of his coworkers, he listed a member of the newspaper staff living in New York City as our sponsor. This man had played this role for several others. Father, mother and my sister also enrolled in a class: English for foreigners. The class was for adults only so I was out of luck.

DPs

Once our applications were filed, we officially became members of a growing throng of displaced persons, or DPs, awaiting transport, and as such we were required to stay in a DP camp, usually some former army barrack. This was a blessing because in this camp we didn't have to pay for room or board, while we were being "processed". This involved medical examinations and interviews. Father spent most of his time filling out forms. Thankfully his lawyer training made that relatively easy, but he always had an English/Czech dictionary at his side as he worked. I think some of the other DPs were assigned aids. This extensive procedure, taking place in Europe, was established after World War II to do away with the emotionally draining processing of immigrants that used to take place in places like Ellis Island, New York. (How awful it must have been for aspiring immigrants if they didn't pass the tests to be forced to turn back after already reaching the shores of what they thought would be their new home? Also how differently are the DPs seeking asylum in the US treated now?)

(For a while I felt a bit cheated thinking we would not be listed in the rosters of the Ellis Island museum. But in 2014 I visited that museum and to my delight found us all listed as arrivals in New York City in January 1950.)

In most of the post war DP camps men and women were segregated. But the camp near Frankfurt, where we were first assigned, housed relatively few DPs, and we were allowed to stay together as a family. We shared a large room with another family. They were from Poland, which was good because mother knew some Polish. With her help, our mutual knowledge of some German and a lot of sign language we got along pretty well. We ate army rations (mostly hash and potatoes) in a cafeteria, where the din of mixed languages was amazing. We used to refer to the different languages by how they sounded to us, e.g. *aquah dahquah* or *ishthili pishthili*. We slept on canvas cots, and shared a bathroom down the hall with several other women. There was a strong smell of disinfectant everywhere, and the only decorations were posters warning about health hazards. There was little privacy. At times male officials even entered our "bedroom" without knocking. (I guess they were still in army mode.) "Don't worry," father tried to encourage us, "we won't be here long."

Because of his legal expertise, father was given a job at the processing headquarters. It didn't bring any income, but it did mean that we received small privileges, like little gifts of chocolate or fresh fruit. Most importantly it meant that he could keep abreast of the progress of our applications. All seemed to be going routinely, until one day father got a shock: We were all approved, except for mother! Father took mother's file to his small desk. On the front page it read: *On the basis of a lesion on her lung, Paula Boruvka is denied entry to the United States.*

Mother had had tuberculosis in the nineteen-twenties, before either of her children were born. She had spent some time then in a sanatorium, and in 1949, when we were DP's, she had had no symptoms for over twenty years. Father held up the Xray included in the file. After calming himself, he knocked on the door of the man in charge. "Sir, please excuse me for troubling you," he said meekly, "but you see my wife's application was not approved because of an old, permanent, and completely inactive scar on her lungs. This scar was exactly the same more than twenty years ago."

"Well, if you can prove that Mr. Boruvka, we will re-examine your wife's application." Father smiled and nodded. He now had a new mission. He must prove it, but how?

DP's were generally not allowed to leave the camp. However, father was permitted to travel to keep in touch with his old friends at the newspaper. (The camp officials did not object to this because father had become a trusted help to them.) On the afternoon of the day he found out about mother's rejection, he went to his friends at the paper for advice. He said nothing to mother. (He probably would have sheltered her from this even under normal circumstances, but lately she had become so high strung that she suffered daily headaches.) His friends at the newspaper advised him to contact a Czech physician, living in Frankfurt. Father must have been genuinely nervous as he rode the streetcar through the scarred streets of Frankfurt, thinking about how often he had worked to overcome legal obstacles that were devastating to the lives of others, never imagining that one day he would be in a similar situation.

"Explain to the officials that the lesion is just an old scar and not a sign of active tuberculosis," the old physician said.

"I tried to tell them, but they said I have to prove it!"

"Hmm," the physician said nodding, and then asked: "Has your wife been sleeping well?" Father nodded, "and her appetite is good?"

"As good as it can be on the DP camp diet."

"There has been no loss of weight?"

"No."

"Bring your wife to my office next week," the grey-haired physician said. (Father felt a ray of hope.) "Come, I want to show you something," he continued and led father into an adjacent room that was crammed with old equipment. In one corner stood an antique looking machine with a glass screen.

"When did you say your wife had TB?"

"Around 1922," Father answered.

"And she has had no signs or symptoms since then?"

"None!"

The physician smiled. "Good, I think I know a way to convince the bureaucrats. You see this is an X-ray machine that was in wide use in the 20's. All we have to do is photograph your wife's lungs with it and the authorities will not be able to tell that it isn't an old picture."

The privilege of leaving the DP camp did not apply to any of us beside father. So father had to devise some sort of unusual circumstance to allow mother to do this. As it happened a member of the staff at the paper where father once worked died that very week, and father was able to say to the camp officials that he and his wife wanted to attend that man's funeral.

I was left in my sister's care and to amuse us father brought us a Red Cross package. These packages were sent from the US to cheer up the DP's. There were never enough of them to go around. We opened it up and laid out the contents on the olive-green blanket of our bed. There were samples of various toiletries: shampoo, soap, mouthwash and toothpaste."What's this?" I asked picking up a stick of deodorant.

"It's an American obsession," smirked my sister. "They are always worried about how they smell."

My attention then focussed on the one item in the package I really liked. It was a small plastic pin in the shape of a blue cartoon bird. It was just like the little birds that perched on Snow White's finger, in the Disney film we had seen in Prague. "Oh, can I have this? I pleaded.

"Sure, squirt," Shari answered on her way to the shower to test the new shampoo.

The fake X-ray proved successful and we hurried to get ready to go to a new DP camp near Bremenhaven, the large sea port from which the ship, to which we were assigned, was to sail. Then another blow descended: The official at the DP headquarters looked pained when he addressed father: "I am really sorry to have to tell you this, but the American sponsor you listed has refused to vouch for you and your family!" Father was hurt and embarrassed. He couldn't understand it. Although he did not know this wealthy American, of Czech extraction, this man had helped many Czech immigrants, and was recommended to him by his good friends at the paper. All the people at the paper were equally dumbfounded.

"Don't you know anyone in the States who could be your sponsor?" asked his friends at the paper.

Father searched his brain, "Well there is a former client of mine living in New York. I think he owns a restaurant."

"Perfect!" beamed the chief and pulled down a very large telephone directory from his extensive collection of directories. It was the Manhattan phone book. "What's his name?"

"Dubsky."

"Hmmm, luckily it is not a very common name," there are only three Dubskys listed here," he said, as he ran his finger down one of the pages. Then without hesitation he picked up the phone and dialed. Father looked on in awe. "Mr. Dubsky?...... are you originally from Prague?" he said in English, and then after a pause continued in Czech: "I have someone here you may remember, Dr. Svatopluk Boruvka..."The chief listened for some time and then he handed the phone to father. "Speak to him he is anxious to talk to you!"

This Mr. Dubsky, his wife and daughter were helped by father to get out of Czechoslovakia before the Nazis became virulent. Mr. Dubsky filed an affidavit stating that he would sponsor us, and since he owned a restaurant in Manhattan he was a very acceptable sponsor because he could promise to employ us, new immigrants, if the necessity arose. With this second obstacle removed, we packed our few belongings into a wooden foot locker on which my sister neatly lettered S. Boruvka c/o Mr. Dubsky, followed by the Dubsky's Manhattan address, United States of America.

My family thought that our original US sponsor backed out because of efforts made by our relative, Vera, who deeply resented Father. Her feelings of hostility against my father stemmed from her parents' divorce, which father had managed, as lawyer. But mainly, I think, she was so embittered because of the horror that Hitler afflicted on Vera's mother: She was Jewish and along with millions of others, she died in a Nazi concentration camp. I think that Vera mistakenly thought that father could have done something to save her, because father was still practicing law at that time. After the Communist takeover, Vera was so set on revenge for wrong she felt my father was implicit in, that she pulled all the strings she could: So with the help of her husband, who was then an active government official, she succeeded in persuading that original would-be sponsor from supporting us.

Much later, I learned, from a distant relative, Eva*, who came from the same branch of our family as Vera, that Vera's married name was Prochaskova, and that she had become an artist, using an art form popular in Prague: marionette theater.

> **We found Eva and her husband Denis in 1963 through a saga that seems unbelievable:*

In 1938, before the start of World War II, relatives of my uncle's divorced wife, Vera, sent a young daughter, named Eva to

England for her safety. I learned what happened to her after that only after she and I became friends, in the 1960s. I am telling it here in sequence:

During her English exile, Eva married a fellow Czech named Denis. After the war, Eva and Denis immigrated to Australia, and subsequently to the US. They settled in the San Francisco Bay Area.

In 1963, while I was about to move from New York to California to study at UC Berkeley, a good, platonic friend, of mine, named Jeffrey, made acquaintance with Eva and Denis as follows:

Jeffrey was living in the Bay Area in California, where he became friendly with a topless dancer in San Francisco. (This form of art and entertainment was particularly popular there then.) Jeffrey was very protective of this girl and would always accompany her at the nightclub when she performed. One evening my relatives, Eva and Denis, visited that nightclub and after the performance, which featured Jeffrey's friend, they asked her to join them for a drink. She and her guardian, Jeffery, came to sit at their table. During their conversation Jeffrey asked where Eva and Denis were from because he had noticed their accent. "Well," they answered," we are originally from Prague."

Jeffrey smiled: "I have a friend from Prague, named Radmila Boruvka."

Eva became ecstatic, and said: "This is a relative of mine, you must give me her contact information."

Jeffrey frowned and refused. (This was a time of cold war unease everywhere.)

"Well, please give her my name and address," Eva retorted after she wrote that information down.

Jeffrey dutifully sent that slip of paper to me and when I showed it to my father, he immediately picked up the phone: "Evicko, is it really you?" said Father in Czech and a happy reunion eventually ensued, which was particularly fortunate because I soon moved to Berkeley. Eva and Denis became my good friends. In fact they hosted a reception in their house after my wedding, at which Eva was my matron of honor.

Immigrants

After all our processing was finished, we were officially classified as immigrants. My father had made sure that we were all registered as wanting US citizenship. We sent our foot-locker, packed with the few worldly things we still possessed, ahead to the sponsors, the Dubskys, and we were moved by train to a seaport, called Bremerhaven.

Shari and I wanted to explore this new city, but there was too much, post-war chaos for sightseeing. Mother and Shari wrote letters (mother to her sister and Shari to her boyfriend). Each used an alias agreed upon before our departure. This was done to protect the recipients, after all we were now criminal escapees from our native land. Father tried to maintain some standing with the authorities. He presented a letter of recommendation from the commandant in the Frankfurt camp, and was appointed to help a team making sure the galley of our ship-to-be, was filled with all needed food and supplies. Father's fluent German was useful, despite his broken English.

The Bremerhaven DP camp was even more primitive than those we had before, but our spirits were much better. Men and women had separate sleeping quarters, but we met father at meals where we met a young Czech man who was heading for Australia. He told us that he chose Australia because he was a keen tennis player and he knew the sport was very big there. "Besides, it sounds interesting," he said grinning. True, I thought, but so does New York!

At last the day came when we were to board an army cargo ship, named General Howze, which was refitted to handle several hundred immigrants.

It was December on the North Sea, and we bundled ourselves into sweaters and winter coats. We had knitted hats, scarves and gloves that mother had purchased in Frankfurt. The ship was not as large as I had expected. An identical sister ship, named General Greeley, was docked next to General Howze.

As we and the other immigrants filed off a bus that carried us to the dock, the smell of the sea and the noise of many people milling around were disorienting. We climbed a shaky gangplank in single file. Shari was the first of us in line. Father carried my duffel bag and mother held my hand. At the top we were to be given cards with the number and location of our bunks. "Open your blouse!" commanded a sailor at the top of the gangplank, when Shari reached him. She knew enough English to understand, but she couldn't believe her ears.

"Pardon?" she asked squinting at him.

"Come on, we haven't got all day" he yelled impatiently, and gestured at unbuttoning his uniform. She did as she was told and he threw a handful of pesticide powder at her. Father complied also.

Mother was already preparing her own top, when she looked at the sailor imploringly and said: "NO bitte!" gesturing toward me. Mother's hand was over my mouth and she held my head close to her body as if this might protect me from the acrid smell. The sailor looked over at his superior, who shrugged and gestured to let us pass. This humiliation left us speechless for a while. We stopped before a large diagram of the ship, where father showed us where our bunks were located and how to get to them. Mother, Shari and I were on one side of the ship and father on the other. Shari sketched a small map on an envelope and we went to place our duffel bags on our bunks. We agreed to reunite with father in a lounge in about a half hour.

USS GENERAL R. L. HOWZE AP-134

We descended small metal stairs. Further and further down the air got warmer a staler. We finally reached our designated area, which was filled with stuffy air and bunks as far as we could see. Mother and Shari surveyed the place, and then they just turned around and we quickly reascended to the lounge to meet father. It wasn't easy maneuvering the duffel bags, which now seemed bulkier and heavier than before, since we were moving against the rest of the foot traffic.

When we sat down in the lounge, I was tired and discouraged. Shari noticed my downturned mouth. "Come on," she said taking my hand. "Let's check out the sea." We walked out on the deck and leaned over the railing on the side of the ship away from the dock.

"Is this the ocean?" I asked looking at the water edging the horizon.

"No, the ocean is much bigger!" answered Shari and steered me back to the lounge. I had a hard time imagining the ocean being wider, since the sea stretched as far as I could see, so I thought of it being bigger vertically. This translated in my mind into height instead of depth and filled me with dread.

When father joined us and heard our complaints, he didn't hesitate to try changing our accommodations. His experience in dealing with officials and his polite insistence paid off, and we were moved from deck E to deck C. The furnishings were the same, nothing but bunks stacked, three high, but the air felt fresher. We parked our bags at the foot of each bunk. (I wanted to sleep on the topmost one but mother would only permit me to go as high as the middle one.)

When we returned to the outside, our ship was passing the English White Cliffs of Dover.

It was the last land we were to see for the next ten days.

After supper in a cafeteria with long, metal tables, we returned to the outside deck. It was already dark and my eyes were drawn to the water below, separated by the passage of the ship and illuminated from the ship's windows below. It was a beautiful, translucent green, but the idea of the enormous depth of the ocean that my sister had told me about earlier, made me nervous.

Down a narrow hall, from our sleeping quarters, there were communal showers and small sinks lining the wall in a large wash room. Even though we eventually overcame much of our shyness, we always took showers early in the morning, when only a few fellow, female passengers were up. The toilets were located in the lowest part of the ship, where you could see the slanting of the walls that formed the ship's keel. Even the toilets were communal, i.e. there were no stalls. I preferred going down there only in the middle of the night, when usually no one else was around.

In the first few days we spent much of our time on the outside deck. (Having come from a landlocked country, we were making up for never having seen the ocean before.) The water stretching toward the horizon looked strangely solid, with waves etching it in interesting patterns. We could see the General Greeley ship that was moving with us some distance away. As time passed we noticed this sister ship was bobbing up and down, more and more. It would rise high above us on a huge wave and then disappear behind another wave. As we watched and thought that our own ship must be behaving the same way, we all became, almost simultaneously, seasick.

Seasickness is a strange thing. It makes you lose all focus and a heaving feeling dominates your entire being. Mother and Shari had it the worst. They just laid on their bunks refusing to move. I threw up only once: When my feeling of nausea was strongest, I managed to get to the deck. The ship was in the midst of a storm. The side of the ship getting the brunt of the storm was roped off to prevent passengers from going there. I didn't want anyone to see me vomit, so I ducked under the ropes to the forbidden side. There, holding tightly to the rail lining the wall, I spilled the contents of my stomach on the deck, where they were promptly washed away by ocean spray. After that I felt better and was not seasick again for the rest of the trip. Father was also soon normal, so he and I spent a lot of time together. We ate in the cafeteria, while mother and Shari refused to come to meals, and we discussed everything from the workings of the ship to what it might be like in the U.S.

One day as I was passing the windows of the ship's kitchen, a steward's face appeared in one of the small circles. He had a black face, the first black person I ever saw, and he said something to me with a wide grin. I could not understand his

English, but when he handed me an orange, I grinned back. After that, I would pass that port hole at the same time each day, and often the same steward would be there with an orange to give me. It meant a lot to me. The bright color of the fruit made a wonderful contrast to the dirty white of the ship and the gray of the ocean and sky. I would hold the orange for a long while before peeling it and sharing it with father.

Shari and mother became so debilitated and dehydrated from their many trips to a sink down the hall that they could hardly move. Then suddenly what seemed like a heavenly aroma made my sister sit up. "What is that smell?" she said to mother, who had also noticed it. They looked in its direction to find a lady opening a jar of pickled herring. They had talked to this lady before, and now they descended on her like hungry birds.

"Oh yes, herring, pickled, with no cream is the best way to beat seasickness," the lady said with a smile. "My husband owned a fishing boat and used this method with all the rookies."

"Amazing," exclaimed mother, "just the smell made me feel better."

"Please understand," continued the lady, "I don't have enough of this to share. I could let you have some of juice if you like."

It was remarkable that even a few spoonfuls of the juice revived the two women. Soon they were on their way to the cafeteria and the perpetual sausage and sauerkraut was delicious to them.

With Shari's revival I gained another companion for ship exploring. We found our way to an upper deck that housed a small movie theatre, which to our delight showed movies now and then. When I watched Doris Day sing "My Dream Is Yours." I thought she was the most beautiful woman in the world.

The ship put out a mimeographed newsletter for the immigrants, and father suggested that Shari draw a banner design for it. She drew our ship plowing through the water toward a sunburst that featured the Statue of Liberty backed by the American flag. The editor loved it. Shari pretended that she thought it was kitschy but I could tell she was proud of it too.

Our voyage took ten days because we had to loop around a large mid-Atlantic storm, which gave our small ship a rough ride.

At last we sighted a glimpse of land on the distant horizon. Mother cleaned everything in sight. Our packing didn't take long, and we didn't have to do any choosing as to what to wear. My sister was more annoying than usual, fussing with her hair. She didn't want to wear her knitted hat, but when she emerged onto the windy deck she appreciated it. We stood there amidst the throng of other immigrants, watching the buildings of Staten and Ellis Islands pass. Then all eyes reverted on the large, pale green statue on the left. Father surprised me as we passed it by bending down and kissing the top of my head. (He was not usually so demonstrative.) The ship pulled up on the west Side of Manhattan. Great buildings dominated the view. On the dock, yellow machines with arms and mouths like dinosaurs, were moving boxes.

We walked down a narrow gangplank and into a warehouse-like building. The confusion of milling people was eased as we were greeted by an elegant lady, who spoke our language! I was asked to sign next to my name on a long list.

Then we rode in a big car through Manhattan. The car belonged to the nice lady's husband. They were our sponsors. The big signs in Times Square, were impressive but I did not like one of them, which noisily puffed smoke.

We settled in a dingy hotel overnight. In the morning my parents made a large breakfast of eggs, fried potatoes and orange juice. This was different from the usual breakfast of tea and some buns.

Then our sponsor drove us past very big, grey buildings to a yellow house in the suburbs. We were greeted by a wonderful dog, named Napoleon, who became a good friend to me. Soon we moved into that house with the dog and an old invalid lady. It was a happy arrangement: mother cooked and took care of that lady, and father went to look for a job.

Our Lives in Our New Country
==========================

My sister, Shari, was at that awkward late, teenage stage when our family upheaval happened. An early sign of her stress appeared in her over-consuming fried chicken and milkshakes in that US army commissary in Frankfurt. Her resulting slight plumpness exasperated the usual trials after she entered high school in the US, where despite her aptitude for languages she had issues about communication. She once told me that there was a slim French girl at her school that made her jealous: "Her exotic French accent is much better than the guttural Czech accent." In a move to help her fitting in she changed her given name, Sarka, to Shari.

She was talented in art and music, so after high school she entered Pratt Institute of Art in Brooklyn, where among students that shared her sensitivities she grew happier. Then, upon graduating with a BA, she got a commercial graphics job, doing mostly routine paste-ups. At that time, to lift her spirits, she started singing lessons, and this became a turning point in her life:

Her singing teacher was on the faculty of Julliard School of Music, and with her help, Shari enrolled there. Consequently, we all enjoyed wonderful student performances in which my sister showed off her acting ability along with her voice. I particularly remember when she sang the lead in Massenet's *Werther*.

Thanks to her well-received singing and acting experience at Julliard, she succeeded in winning a Fulbright Scholarship to continue study of opera in Europe. Subsequently, she was hired by an Opera repertoire company in Wuppertal, Germany.

She never described to me her success during the twenty five years she spent as an opera singer in Europe. I learned about it from newspaper clippings that mother saved. Only once Shari told me how much it all meant to her in a letter she wrote in a dressing room of the Vienna State Opera, where she sang as a guest.

In Germany she married a fellow Opera singer, with whom she had a baby daughter. Their occupations demanded a lot of travel, which made family life difficult and their marriage ended in divorce. Our parents (then just retired) went to live near Shari in Germany to help with her child.

After father died, and Shari's little girl grew so she could largely take care of herself, mother returned to the US to live near me.

Shari eventually also moved back to the US, where she got a job teaching voice at a university in the US state of Alabama.

She settled with her daughter in the University town of Montevallo, where she enjoyed seeming to be relatively exotic. She once told me: "The Germans and the US Southerners have something in common: they both feel shame for the past wrongs of their countrymen.

My mother was in her late forties when she was forced to exchange a comfortable life full of music and art for one with a different culture and language.

Our first refuge in the New York suburbs came to end when everyone in the family (except me) developed ties to something within the City of New York itself: Father secured a job in a bank as a mid-level clerk, Shari was accepted at Pratt, and mother got a job as a pastry cook in a Manhattan restaurant

Brooklyn then became the logical place for us to live, not only because of the nearness of Shari's college, but also because it was cheaper than comparable places in Manhattan. I recall a knot in my chest when we first walked through the apartment in Brooklyn that my parents had secured. The place smelled of sloppily-applied, white paint, and was a big contrast to our grand home in Prague and even to our recent home in the suburbs. However, Mother had nothing but praises for it. What I did not comprehend at the time was that to her, this was a step toward restoring our former life: at last our own place, which we could fill with our own things.

Luckily there was the St. Vincent DePaul Thrift Store, where we secured most of the imperishable things we needed: dishes, pots and pans and second-hand furniture. Mother tirelessly scanned the store for anything that had a semblance of former glory: a threadbare Persian rug, glass bowls with etched designs, a mirror in a gilded frame.

Mother obtained her first paying job with the help of that friend who had been our sponsor in the immigration process: She became the pastry cook at a fancy Manhattan restaurant, where she made deserts and appetizers, putting to use the skills she had learned in Prague by watching our hired help at holidays and parties. The job actually paid more than father's, but it was a hard: She had to commute on the subway and always arrived home from work around two AM. From the subway station she had to walk on a deserted Brooklyn street to reach our apartment house. On one of those late nights, she was attacked by a pickpocket. He grabbed her by the throat and took her entire week's pay, about $ 70. (She was always paid in cash. I have often wondered how this robber knew to attack her just on her payday.) Mother's employer actually cheated her because he did not report her as his employee for years. As a result, when she retired, she had not accumulated as much social security as she should have. After that late night street attack mother claimed she lost her singing voice.

Mother's attempts to surround herself with reminders of her previous life, like that rug from St. Vincent's, were not harmful, but later her sense of loss developed into hostility toward any person, who in her mind was an obstacle to the success of her family. The following is relatively insignificant, but I think it exemplifies her state of mind: I remember being embarrassed as she lashed out at a person who apparently unintentionally stepped in front of her while getting on a bus.

Fifty-three year old father, was perhaps effected more than any of us by the upheavals we endured. He had been an admired defense lawyer in Prague for several decades, (I was too young to accompany my sister then, but she told me how she loved going to court to hear father speak), but as an immigrant, who spoke heavily accented English and whose real skills were only using his mind, getting a job was difficult. So to take care of his family father became a chauffeur and a handy-man. Eventually, he managed to land a position as clerk in the letters of credit department of a big bank. This allowed him to put to use at least some of his knowledge in languages and law, but he was always under a boss, about half his age.

I know he dreamed about other things at first. When I was a student at NYU, I suggested to him to go see the law school administration at that University. Although he never talked about it to me, he may have looked into it. In retrospect I realize that it was a foolish suggestion for me to make, considering his age, his thick accent and the fact that his family needed his income.

Despite everything, father never lost his gentleness and sincere interest in anything I brought up for discussion, even esoteric issues in science.

I was ten years old when I was enrolled in a public school within walking distance of that yellow house in the suburbs. I started to call myself Roddy to fit in better with my friends, but officially I always remained Radmila.

At first, school was a source of trial and embarrassment for me: I was placed in the third grade despite my advanced age of ten. The other students seemed to shun me, and the teachers treated me like an idiot. For example, one day my fellow students were asked to read some cards to test for colorblindness. I was eager to find out if I was colorblind, but they wanted to leave me out of being tested, probably because they thought I couldn't pronounce all the English names of the numbers on the cards. They tried to push and lead me away. I said "NO". So they let me try. Now I know that I am not colorblind.

On another day the lesson was about continents. All the other students tried to point out the continents on a map of the world, but usually they missed at least one. I knew the English pronunciation of Asia, Africa etc. so I raised my hand. The other students snickered. But I had the last laugh because I pointed to and named all the continents correctly on the map as well as on a globe. I particularly remember being careful to pronounce the "c" in Antarctica.

Each day at home, after I finished my homework I would stare out the window, wistfully gazing at kids playing in a neighbor's yard. Then one day one of the neighbor girls rang our bell. "Can the girl with the red kerchief come out to play?" she said, and my loneliness was over. Finding friends, and the selfless care of my parents, settled my world into relative comfort. I learned English by assimilation, and eventually no one could easily label me, foreign.

After that I can honestly say that I did not suffer any further problems stemming from my immigrant status. At least that's how I perceive it now in my old age.

(The only reminder of my immigrant status that I experienced later occurred when I was planning to go to graduate school. I applied to Harvard, UC Berkeley and Penn State. Harvard wanted proof that I was fluent in English. When a professor, who was my mentor at the City University of New York, learned about Harvard's request, he became furious: "How could they think that you excelled here without fluency in English?" he said.)

Today I feel that unlike the rest of my family, I succeeded to become Americanized, especially after I married my wonderful, American-born husband, Bob.

I also realize now how much I owe to my doting parents: My sister and I never felt any lack, e.g. cost was never considered when we wanted to attend prestigious colleges; or when I moved to California mother spending hours ironing and packing my clothes into a large trunk; or when Shari needed help with baby care, parents did not hesitating to pack up and move to her. (They even sent their furniture to me, all the way to California.)

I also never realized what a financial burden we had been, until one day while I was visiting my parents in New York, father asked me to help him in securing a loan. He introduced me to a clerk interviewer saying that I was his daughter, studying in California. "So you're the one needing money?" asked the clerk amiably. I just smiled, even though I was baffled because by that time I was on a fellowship and had not asked for any more money from parents. Father had not explained anything to me before this interview. I guess he relied on my ability to perceive things with discretion. He was apparently hoping that using me as "collateral" would push the loan through.

So now, sitting in my house and garden, contemplating my accomplished, healthy and thoroughly American children, I hope that my parents, in heaven, hear my most grateful praises.

PART II

My Biology Research Career

I have always been interested in things scientific. For Example, as a child I was fond of playing with small statues of dinosaurs, for which I would try building natural settings; and after we moved to Brooklyn, and I finally got my own bedroom, I painted its walls two beautiful shades of green, to express my love of plants.

In college I chose to major in biology, not only because I loved the beauty of plants and animals, but also because I appreciated the technical aspects of biochemistry and physics that produce their structure. Happily the required freshman biology course at NYU was taught by a talented, senior professor, named Douglas Marsland. Dr. Marsland had written a great text for that course, and I devoured most of that textbook even before my first semester started in the fall of 1954.

Later I specialized in genetics, probably because during my undergraduate years the entire science world became fascinated with advances in understanding inheritance:

A Short History of the Science of Genetics

For centuries, inheritance was only an unreliable tool for agriculture and animal husbandry, but in the nineteenth century, the science of genetics was born thanks to Gregor Mendel, an Augustinian monk and a teacher of mathematics, who recognized and formulated basic laws of inheritance after meticulously crossing garden pea plants. Mendel's pivotal paper was published in 1866 in a botanical journal, where it laid dormant for thirty years. It was simultaneously discovered by three independent European botanists, Hugo de Vries, Carl Correns and Erich von Tschermak, in 1900.

During the first quarter of the twentieth century, Thomas Hunt Morgan with his students and colleagues at Columbia University formulated other basic laws of inheritance, including gene linkage and crossing over, and demonstrated that radiation causes mutations. They did this using the prolific fruit fly, *Drosophila,* which can be grown in small milk bottles on a layer of porridge and yeast.

T.H. Morgan was originally an entomologist. Interestingly, it was Morgan's wife and co-worker, Lilian Vaughan Morgan, who drew her husband's attention to Drosophila after she noticed the white eye phenotype among normally red eyed wild flies. (I learned this from Dr. Curt Stern, who had been Morgan's student.)

How Molecular Biology Came to Dominate Genetics

A new field, called Molecular Biology, started when it was proven that the macromolecule, DNA, controls heredity. Focus on molecular aspect now dominates biology to such an extent that in some universities (notably UC Berkeley) related departments have been reorganized.

In the 1860s physician and biologist, Friedrich Meischer, showed DNA to be a major component of chromosomes, the then known carriers of inherited information (1); In 1952 Alfred Hershey and Martha Chase proved that DNA was the genetic material, by using isotope labeling of a bacteriophage (2); and In 1958 James Watson and Francis Crick published a beautifully logical and functional model of the structure of DNA, for which they later received a Nobel prize.

Watson's and Crick's coworker, Dr. Rosalind Franklin crystallized isolated DNA, and analyzed this crystal with X-rays. One of her X-ray diffraction photographs convinced Watson and Crick of the helical nature of DNA. Franklin never received proper recognition for her indispensable work.

In 1958 I graduated from NYU, with a Bachelor of Arts degree…(I guess NYU administrators were more impressed with my taking one elective philosophy course, than my otherwise science-filled transcript.), and I decided to continue my study of biology at Brooklyn College, where I had been hired as a teaching assistant to help with basic biology laboratories.

Brooklyn College had a vibrant group that at that time used the yeast, *Saccharomyces cerevisiae,* to analyze aspects of inheritance, such as gene crossing over between chromosomes during cell division.

Yeast is handy for genetic studies because it can be easily grown in petri dishes, where it can exist as haploid cells, which can be made to combine in a specific medium to produce diploid cells. In turn these diploid cells, revert by meiosis to being haploid, when grown in another specific medium.

Under the guidance of that vibrant genetics lab, I used yeast for my master's thesis research, in which I tried to shed some light on the synthesis of purines.

Purines are a key component of nucleic acids, including DNA.

Working out a synthetic pathway in any organism is important since all living organisms ultimately have a common ancestor. Therefore, a key metabolic pathway in one species is usually similar to that pathway in many other species.

I remember posting a big poster chart on my wall, which recorded the known synthetic and anabolic pathways of living cells. It was entitled "Intermediate Metabolism" and did not specify in any particular species.

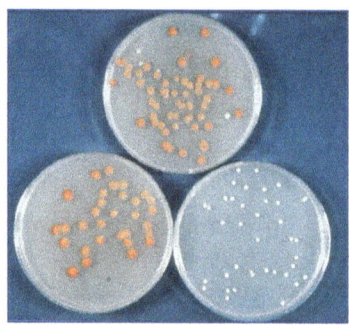

Colonies of yeast on petri dishes

There are several variants of, *S. Crevisciae,* that have a bright red color. This is due to their accumulation of red intermediates in the purine synthetic pathway. These accumulations result from mutations that block different steps in the synthesis of purines. (Nevertheless, they can be grown in petri dishes, if you supply them with the purine end product.) From these each accumulated product can be identified by paper chromatography.

Paper chromatography employs a solvent moving by diffusion across blotting paper on which extracts are dotted. Because various molecules in cell extracts have different solubilities, the solvent movement carries them at different rates to different distances from the origin, thereby separating them. (Incidentally a similar concept is used in gel electrophoresis, which I used later to separate protein products for part of my PhD thesis.)

I could produce the needed extracts easily because my thesis advisor, Dr. Norman Eaton, had devised a method for fracturing frozen yeast cells, with a metal pistons and a large press.

In my paper chromatograms, I managed to find some of the purine precursors that accumulate in different mutant yeast strains. (The natural red color of these products helped.) Originally I had hoped to rank the mutations (thus defining the metabolic pathway of purines) by crossing their hosts.

However, after I passed an oral exam and my efforts with paper chromatography were accepted, I happily applied to become a graduate student at UC Berkeley, with dreams of solving questions about gene control.

How Genes Control Development

During the 1960s many "Molecular Biologists", did not focus on whole organisms or even on intact cells, but instead manipulated isolated molecules. The most common sources of their biologically active molecules were bulk cultures of mammalian cells or of the bacterium, *E.coli*. Many enzymes and the three RNAs that are key in protein synthesis, were isolated and made to "read" DNA in vitro. Artificially synthesized nucleotide polymers, as well as some natural DNA, were used to crack the genetic code (3).

A comparatively solitary but crucial insight into gene regulation in whole cells was published at that time, by Francois Jacob and Jacques Monod (4). They studied changes in gene expression, when *E. Coli* is grown on different culture media. They received a Nobel Prize for their work, but such adaptations, are probably different from apparently permanent changes cells make during development in multicellular organisms. I realized that to study this development, I would have to use multicellular organisms.

When one wants to study genetic mechanisms, the choice of the subject organism is crucial. For example, Gregor Mendel, could not have succeeded if the pea plants he studied did not have distinct traits located on a few linkage groups (now called chromosomes). And T.H. Morgan's team at Columbia University could not have demonstrated fundamental phenomena, like crossing over and the effect of radiation on mutation rates, without the tiny and prolific, Drosophila melanogaster flies, which have complex morphology and produce a new generation in weeks, while housed in small milk bottles with a layer of porridge.

Study of development in multicellular organisms, or embryology is a field with a long history: Scientist, in the past had used ingenious experiments, manipulating eggs and embryos of echinoderms and as well as of vertebrates.

When I originally envisioned doing research in Berkeley I wanted to use plants, because I wanted to avoid having to dissect and harm living animals. And I admit that my choice of UC Berkeley was influenced by my awareness of two famous researchers there: Professors Daniel Arnon and Melvin Calvin, who had elucidated the vital, plant process of photosynthesis. Little did I realize that these illustrious professors were largely inaccessible to lowly young freshmen graduate students.

Luckily I found Professor James Fristrom, a member in the Genetics Department at UC, who was using the fly, *Drosophila melanogaster* to study development. *Drosophila*, with its complex morphology, ease of cultivation and genetics, already elegantly studied, seemed to be ideal for this. Dr. Fristrom had come from Rockefeller University in New York, where he had devised a way to isolate fly imaginal discs *en mass*. Importantly, with Fristrom's method these discs were isolated from masses of age synchronized larvae. This was accomplished by placing the trays of food into large plastic cages where *Drosophila* adults were housed. Then the adult flies readily placed fertilized eggs into this food, from which the resulting larvae were isolated.

Imago is the term for adult in metamorphosing insects. Imaginal discs are compact structures of cells within fly larvae that develop into adult parts after metamorphosis.

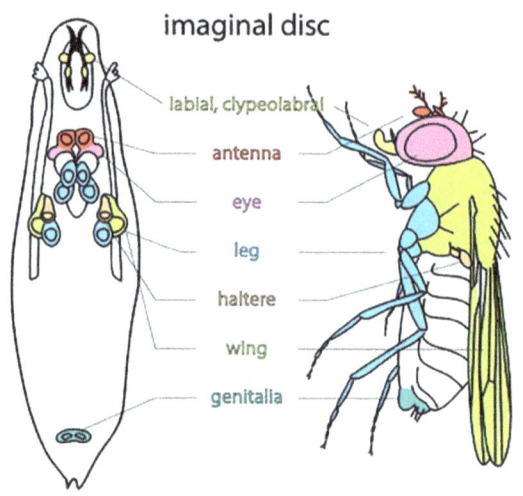

larva → metamorphosis → adult

Previous studies of imaginal discs, that involved meticulous micro-dissections, indicated that imaginal discs were programmed to become specific parts of the adult, but now, having large volumes of these discs, a biochemical study of how discs are programmed and triggered at metamorphosis became feasible. Happily, Dr. Fristrom accepted me as his graduate student and I had had no objection to manipulating flies, within reason.

At the time when I joined the Fristrom lab, ecdysone, the steroid hormone that triggers insect metamorphosis could only be isolated from huge quantities of insect larvae, and only one, well-endowed lab at Harvard University was able to accomplish this. Consequently, getting even small amounts of the purified hormone was difficult.

I happened to learn somehow that a Czech scientist, Dr. Herout, an expert in phytochemistry, was involved in the isolation of ecdysterone, a steroid closely related to ecdysone from common fern plants. Because of my Czech heritage I did not hesitate to write to Dr. Herout, who graciously sent us a large quantity of this chemical, in a plain white envelope. (I suspect that the fact that Czechoslovakia was then in the grips of a repressive Communist government had something to do with his magnanimous gift.)

I speculate that the advantage plants gain in producing ecdysterone is that it upsets the hormonal balance of insect larvae that feed on these plants. (Such imbalance stops the predator insects' development.)

Ecdysterone, a steroid, is now commercially available. I'm not sure if it is still isolated from botanical sources. Significantly, even in animals, including humans, steroid hormones influence cell growth and gene activity.

My PhD Thesis

Having a large source of isolated target tissues (imaginal discs) as well as a good quantity the trigger hormone (ecdysterone), I set out to study changes in RNA synthesis associated with metamorphosis. I succeeded in showing that the hormone increases bulk RNA synthesis in imaginal discs, and that the optimal ecdysterone concentration for that *in vitro* effect is within physiological range.

Since bulk accumulation of chemicals can be effected by dynamics of product stability and precursor availability, I showed by labeling studies that both these factors did NOT influence my measurements as follows:

1. <u>No effect on RNA stability:</u> RNA in imaginal discs was first labeled by exposing isolated discs to radioactive RNA precursors. Then these labeled discs were separated into two batches and incubated further with or without ecdysterone. No effect on the gradual loss of the labeled RNA was observed when further RNA synthesis was inhibited by Actinomycin D.

2. <u>No effect on the size of precursor pools:</u> Imaginal discs were incubated with or without ecdysterone and exposed to radioactive RNA precursors. The amount of label in intracellular precursor pools was the same whether the discs received ecdysterone or not.

I was granted a PhD in early 1970.

My husband, Bob, had received his PhD in 1968. Luckily he managed to get a temporary teaching appointment at Berkeley, which allowed me to finish my thesis, before we moved to Honolulu, where he had successfully lined up a postdoctoral grant to study endemic Hawaiian birds.

How Ecology Influenced my Research

When we moved to Hawaii, I went to see Dr. Elmo Hardy, who had been recommended to me by my professors at Berkeley. Dr. Hardy was at that time studying insects, endemic to the Hawaiian Islands. He in turn graciously urged me to go see Dr. Hampton Carson, who was famous for many studies of genetics and evolution, and who serendipitously was just at that time moving to the University of Hawaii to head the "Hawaiian *Drosophila* Project". Dr. Carson listened to my history and showed me the beautiful giant polytene chromosomes he was studying. I proposed to look whether these chromosomes, when freshly dissected from larvae, would react to exposure to ecdysterone, which by that time had become commercially available.

Happily, Dr. Carson arranged for me to become a member of his team.

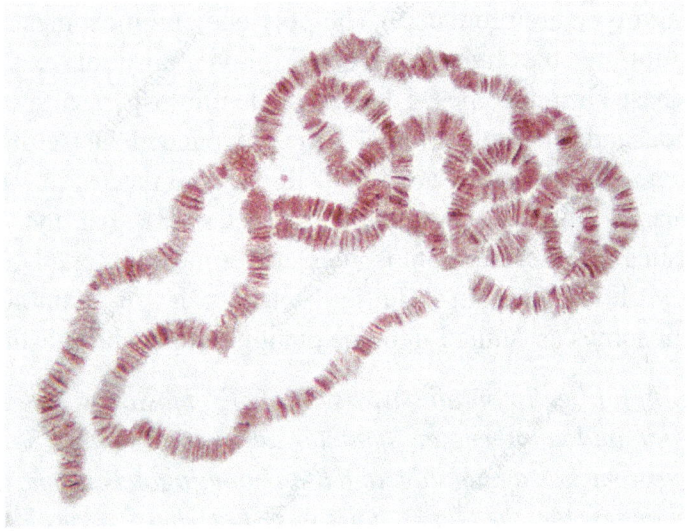

Polytene chromosomes in a salivary gland cell of a Hawaiian Droophila sp.

Polytene Chromosomes

In interphase (i.e. in non-dividing) cells, chromosomes cannot be seen under a light microscope because at that stage the chromosomes are expanded into thin threads.

In Berkeley the genetics graduate students and professors sometimes held informal get-togethers. I recall one of these that featured Dr. Curt Stern, an intellectual son of the founder of Drosophila genetics, T.H. Morgan (referenced above). Dr. Stern, an emeritus lecturer in Berkeley at that time, said: "If you had asked me in the 1920's what I want for Christmas, I would have said: giant chromosomes in which you can actually see genes." And that is in fact what giant polytene chromosomes really are.

During cell division (mitosis), chromosomes become contracted, or packed up, to facilitate their exact apportionment into daughter cells. (This is when chromosomal shapes and sizes we know as the karyotype are produced.) The polytene chromosomes are an exception to the light microscopic invisibility of expanded interphase chromosomes. They are made microscopically visible by thousandfold replications of their expanded DNA threads. Polytene chromosomes are found in specific tissues in various organisms, notably Diptera or true flies (8). All the DNA replicates in these chromosomes are annealed together, i.e. exactly lined up. In addition each pair of homologous chromosomes are united into one giant polytene chromosome.

Each diploid cell contains two sets of chromosomes, one set of paternal and another set of maternal chromosomes. So each chromosome has a homolog, and both homologous chromosomes carry genes for the same functions, but these genes can be different alleles.

Polytene chromosomes are the result of two homologs annealing and replicating their DNA strands thousands of times.

Polytene chromosomes had been first seen in the salivary glands of another fly in 1881, and they were demonstrated in *Drosophila* the 1930's. Such giant polytene chromosomes are found in mature, non-dividing cells, which usually have secretory function, just as the larval salivary glands have.

Many species (9) of the tiny fruit flies, *Drosophilae,* are found, distributed all over the world, and the banding patterns of their polytene chromosomes have been used to track their evolution. Although all *Drosophila* species appear to be related, there are many obvious, "scramblings" of the banding of their polytene chromosomes, i.e. translocations (the movement of a section of a chromosome to another place in the same or different chromosome) and inversions (the sequence of bands is moved "head to foot" so to speak). Sill, such scrambling are not seen frequently, mainly because they must not interfere with the smooth functioning of the genetic material for their host to survive. So the relatively rare chromosomal changes that do persist can be a way of tracing how the various species of *Drosophila* are related.

Amazingly nearly two thirds of the 1500 Drosophila species known worldwide, are endemic to the relatively tiny Hawaiian Archipelago. This astounding statistic is a consequence of the fact that the Hawaiian Islands were originally sterile, because they were formed by volcanic action, and to the fact that they are the most isolated land mass in the world, located in the middle of the vast Pacific Ocean. So for a small fly to reach them (i.e. in the past before human migration) was very hard. In fact it has been calculated that maybe only one gravid *Drosophila* female was blown into the islands by a huge storm about 26 million years ago and that the progeny of that pioneer fly then evolved (Darwin would have loved it) to become adapted to various habitats, including feeding on different secretions or parts of various plants. Moreover, during their rapid radiating adaptations, they were unimpeded by competition from closely related insects.

Twenty six million years is only at most half the time during which *Drosophila* have been evolving on all the world's big continents, and this amount of time appears not to have been long enough for the Hawaiian *Drosophila* to develop more than a few chromosomal translocations and inversions. As a result, many Hawaiian *Drosophila* are homosequential (i.e. they cannot be distinguished by the banding patterns of their polytene chromosomes). Nevertheless, even these homosequential Hawaiian *Drosophilae* are different species (9), since when flies of one sex and of one species are housed together with flies of the opposite sex and of another species, in bottles with plenty of food, they do not produce fertile adult offspring. Therefore, their divergent morphology and habits in the wild must be due to different gene action, which should be demonstrable by studying the visible gene activity in their polytene chromosome, known as puffing.

In the late nineteenth century it was reported that polytene chromosomes, produce different puffs at various stages of development. Much later these puffs were characterized as RNA, indicating they are consequences of gene activation.

DNA gene sequences are copied into RNA (these are visible as puffs in polytene chromosomes) before the RNA moves into the cytoplasm to be used in protein synthesis or other metabolic processes.

Almost all cells within a multicellular organism (barring mutation) carry basically identical genetic instructions. This is guaranteed by the accuracy of mitosis. Yet obviously different genes are active in different cells, with their widely different morphologies and functions.

I say that almost all cells have identical basic genetic sequences, because it is clear that vertebrate white blood cells, which produce antibodies, have variable DNA regions that code for different specific antibodies.

In Hawaii in 1970 I proposed to study the effect of ecdysterone (which I had used in my PhD thesis) on the puffing activity of isolated polytene chromosomes of late third instar larvae, of different Hawaiian *Drosophilae*.

I showed that an identical region can be activated in two different species, even though in one of these species the chromosomal region involved was inverted. Thus the activation mechanism may not be dependent on a regulator, or if such a regulator exists it must be very close to that active gene.

Then in an interspecific larva* I showed that at the same region where the two participating species had a disparity in puffing (i.e. at the end of the X chromosome, labeled 2 in the photograph below) there was no annealing , and the puffing there was induced by ecdysterone in only one half of the otherwise annealed, homologous chromosomes. It was important to show this in a hybrid larva because only then we could be sure that we were viewing the chromosome at exactly the same stage of development. (Puffs come and go during development). We accomplished this by using an interspecific hybrid.

Please note that an interspecific hybrid cannot metamorphose, but this was enough for the question at hand, because all I needed was the late stage larva of that hybrid.

Dr. Keneth Kaneshiro, who is now the director of the Hawaiian Drosophila project and who was a graduate student at the time, graciously made for me a hybrid larva between the two species known to have different puffing at the end of the X chromosome.

The end to the polytene X chromosome in that interspecific larva was not annealed and only one half of it responded to my in vitro, ecdysterone treatment by puffing. (See my photograph below.)

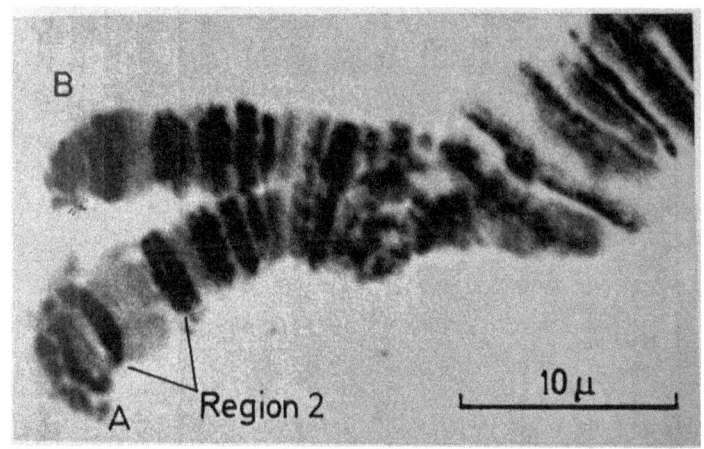

Possible Further Studies

The study of polytene (and perhaps also lampbrush chromosomes, found in amphibian eggs) may give further clues to how DNA is arranged, activated, regulated, and replicated.

We are just learning about the complex network that must regulate gene function in eukaryotes. Dr. Ulrich Clever (11) showed that ecdysterone or ecdysone can induce sequential puffing in polytene chromosomes, indicating that an RNA product of one gene can be required to induce production of RNA by another gene. Many of the puffs of polytene chromosomes are now mapped and given code names. Some regulatory RNAs have been shown to never leave the nucleus. More study of sequential puffing could yield insights in the control of development.

We also don't know why homologous chromosomes anneal to form the polytene chromosomes. This process is probably related to the fact that crossing over between homologs occurs even in regular cell division. Apparently changes in gene coding can prevent this annealing. (As shown in the photograph above, of the end of the X chromosome in my interspecific larva.)

Another mystery lies in the relative speed of DNA replication, necessary for every cell division, since to replicate the DNA double helix must unwind.

What I Did After my Hawaiian Adventure

My husband, Bob, was hired to join the Biology faculty of the University of Pittsburgh and so we left Hawaii. I looked for a job to continue my research career there. Unable to secure one using *Drosophila,* I joined a cancer research unit in a large hospital, thinking that I might be able to apply my understanding of gene action in this field. (After all, cancer is produced by cells acting uncontrollably and that must involve changes in gene action.)

I managed to author, or co-author a dozen research papers in cancer research, but only one of these is somewhat related to my previous work: It shows that feeding vitamin A, which is the same as juvenile hormone in flies, significantly delayed the appearance of tumors in a strain of mice that have a high frequency of cancer. This reinforces my belief that study of reactions in any organism can yield insights into metabolism applicable to all, even humans. (I gave the vitamin A to the mice in their drinking water. Please note that the Vitamin A is chemically identical to juvenile hormone in insects.)

I found that the clinical atmosphere of the community hospital where I worked was not conducive to basic research questions. I remained under supervision of medical doctors and had to use mice as my research subjects. In the latter part of my career there I concentrated on improving the use of antibodies on slides of biopsies, which has been useful in diagnosis.

All my research efforts were never impeded by family duties, which I have always considered most important. I owe this to my wonderful, understanding and supportive husband and to the help my mother gave us while our two sons were babies.

References and footnotes

(1) See a review paper by Ralf Dahm, *Friedrich Miescher and the discovery of DNA, Developmental Biology,* 178: 274-288 (2005).

(2) Hershey A and Chase M *Independent functions of viral protein and nucleic acid in growth of bacteriophage. J.Gen Physiol* 36 (1) 39-56 (1952).

(3) The cracking of the universal genetic code was possible only after the protein synthesis process was understood and its components were isolated: Francis Crick and others produced single base mutations in isolated DNA and analysed what protein like polymers the mutated DNA produced. It is astounding that the triplet genetic code, elucidated in E. coli is found in all living organisms; I mean really all: bacteria, plants, invertebrates and vertebrates, which includes, of course, human beings.

(4) See review paper by Francis Jacob and Jacques Monod, *Genetic Regulatory Mechanisms in the Synthesis of Proteins, J. Mol Bill* 3:318-356 (1961)

(5) A review article by Shiv Patel, *Achievements and Perspectives of Embryology* can be downloaded on line as a free PDF.

(6) Professor Daniel Arnon headed his own separate department, and Professor Melvin Calvin reigned in a new building on campus, which we called "Calvin's Castle.)

(7) The trigger for metamorphosis is actually a shift in the balance of two insect hormones, ecdysone and juvenile hormone. When juvenile hormone concentration is greater than ecdysone, the insect larva molts into a larger larva, but when ecdysone concentration is greater than that of juvenile hormone metamorphosis occurs.

Interestingly ecdysone (and ecdysterone) is a steroid, thus related to the many steroid hormones involved in vertebrate development, and juvenile hormone is a fatty acid derivative, identical in structure to vitamin A. Later during my "cancer research years", I showed that feeding vitamin A to a strain of mice that normally had a high incidence of breast cancer, significantly reduced that incidence.

(8) Each diploid cell contains two sets of chromosomes, one set of paternal and another set of maternal chromosomes. So each chromosome has a homolog, and both homologous chromosomes carry genes for the same functions, but these genes can be different alleles..

Polytene chromosomes are the result of two homologs annealing and replicating their DNA strands thousands of times.

Giant polytene chromosomes have been found in in other organisms beside flies. They appear to arise in tissues whose function is to produce an unusually high abundance of a particular substance.

(9) A species is defined as a group of individuals that can interbreed and produce viable offspring.

(10) R B Raikow, *Puffing in Salivary Gland Chromosomes of Picture-winged Hawaiian Drosophila*; Chromosoma (Berl.) 41, 221-231 (1973).

(11) Ulrich Clever, et al, *The Apparent Requirement of Two Hormones, alpha and beta Ecdysone for Molting Induction in Insects*; Developmental Biology 31: 48-60. (1973).

PART III

My Religion, Blessings and Blunders

As a child in Europe, I had no contact with religion that I can remember. (Our Christmas celebrations were all about presents.) I don't remember us ever attending Mass. Still I was baptized in the Catholic Church, and have a certificate that proves this, which my parents dutifully carried when we immigrated.

<u>My New York Phase</u>

After we settled in Brooklyn, my education concerning Catholicism began when my parents enrolled me in a nearby, Catholic, Grammar School, to be followed by an all-girls, Catholic, High School. (All our teachers were Catholic nuns.)

I made some life-long friends in those schools, dutifully attended Mass, received the sacrament of Confirmation, and even participated in retreats, which I thoroughly enjoyed. However, the church rituals and the preaching I heard then did not really impress me. So I didn't start what I call "practicing" my faith until I entered college in 1954.

As an undergraduate at NYU, I joined the Catholic Newman Club, a staple organization of every secular university, named after Cardinal Newman, who was a convert to Catholicism from Anglicanism in 1845. The Newman Club at NYU at that time was led by a wonderful priest, Father Andrew O'Reilly, who was always willing to discuss any question about religion that came up. (We had regular group meetings called "Pumping the Padre".)

Father O'Reilly and friends that I made at Newman sparked an enthusiasm about religion in me. I somehow became the Newman Club's vice president in charge of religious affairs. (Maybe this happened because nobody else wanted that job.) I don't recall what duties were required for that title. (The vice president in charge of social affairs was much more busy). I only remember posting relevant pictures on our bulletin board, and once organizing a field trip to a nearby church to see a Mass in the Byzantine Rite.

Perhaps the highlight of my NYU days was our Newman Club trip to Europe, which was organized by Father O'Reilly. Father had studied at the Vatican in Rome, and because of his connections there, we were granted a special visit to the Sistine Chapel. The whole trip was wonderful, but the experience of seeing the Sistine Chapel, empty of any tourists except us, was overwhelming.

California and Bob

Following NYU and two years as graduate student and teaching assistant at Brooklyn College (during which I did nothing religious, except attending Sunday Mass), I was accepted at UC Berkeley, in pursuit of a PhD.

I lived independently (for the first time in my life) next to the beautiful UC campus, participated in the anti-war demonstrations of the 60's, and heard inspiring lectures from the faculty and visiting scholars. However, the UC Newman Club did not seem to have much to offer me (there were no discussion groups or even a substantial choir). My courses and duties as assistant in basic biology labs kept me busy, and I started to drift away from Catholicism.

In 1963 I met Bob, a fellow graduate student, who was my partner teaching and running the basic biology laboratories. Bob and I often went on field trips exploring nature in the Bay Area. California was excitingly different from New York, and Bob had a much better knowledge of nature ecology than me. We became more than friends and fell in love. We married two years after we met, at the Oakland Court House.

Bob's family was Jewish, which was never an issue for me or my parents, and over the years I have never found anything that distinguished the ways of Bob's family from what I was used to.

There was a brief period when Bob's parents were upset about him marrying a "shiksa" (non-Jewish girl), but after we all met each other, we developed warm relationships. Even now I still correspond with Bob's surviving sister.

After Bob and I received our PhD's at UC, we did interesting research in Hawaii, (see part II of this book, above) where wonderfully our first son was born in 1970.

Pittsburgh PA and My Mother

In 1971 we moved back to the mainland because Bob had been hired to teach at the University of Pittsburgh, PA.

I managed to find temporary teaching jobs and eventually positions in various research labs. So to help with our toddler son, David, and in happy anticipation of a new baby on the way, my mother came to live near us in 1972. (My father had died that year, and everyone agreed that a change of surroundings would help mother get over her grief.)

With my mother, I returned to weekly attendance at Sunday Mass: At first we would go to a different Catholic Church each week, but eventually we settled on a large, Gothic church near our house. (It looked very much like the church near our apartment in Prague.)

St. Ludmila Church in Prague and SS Peter and Paul Church in Pittsburgh

Happily, SS Peter and Paul Church was run by the Jesuits, and they, living up to the well-deserved Jesuit reputation, never flinched away from any questions or arguments I would pose. I also have fond memories from that time of several retreats with fellow parishioners in beautiful nearby Appalachian Mountains, where we heard inspirational talks from a Jesuit priest, who also heard our confessions. On one of these retreats even my husband, Bob attended.

Bob was never unsympathetic to any aspects of my religion. Much later, when both our children were adult, I felt the need to get married <u>officially by the</u> church (we had been married previously in a civil ceremony.) Bob was happy to indulge me. My Jesuit pastor conducted a simple ceremony at his rectory, accompanied by our two sons and by my elder son's fiancé, who took the picture below, were witnesses.

Posing after our 1989 <u>Church</u> Wedding, with our sons, David (19) and Steven (15, with a white top) next to Father O'Connel, SJ, who performed the ceremony.

<u>This brings me to my present situation in old age and widowhood:</u>

There is a small Catholic Church within walking distance of my house, and nothing short of some hospitalizations can induce me to miss Sunday Mass.

Actually, church activities almost dominate my life now: Our church, called St. David of Wales, has a surprisingly good, classical choir, with which I happily participate in weekly rehearsals and at Sunday Mass. I run a Book Club in which about six friends from the parish meet to read and discuss either a book from the Bible or some book that expands Christian philosophy. Finally another parishioner and I show monthly inspirational movies. I am now in almost* complete agreement with the Catholic Church's teachings.

*See my discussion about birth control, below.

My confidence in the teachings of the Catholic Church, rests on its centuries-old, but still advancing, concept of hierarchical structure, which importantly promotes unity.

I admit that there have been appalling abuses done in the name of the Church in the past: the Crusades, the Inquisition, martyrdom by burning supposed heretics (such as that of the Czech, reformer, Jan Hus), to name just some of the public ones, and I appreciate that over centuries, scholars and saints have tried to stop these abuses. Unfortunately, some reformers, like Martin Luther, forgot the basic structure Jesus had founded, and threw out "the baby with the bathwater."

The teachings of the Catholic Church have been and are proclaimed by a well educated group of scholars called the Magisterium, which strives to base its decrees on scholarship and sound philosophy.

Having a central source of scholarly teaching is lacking for most Protestant Churches, which, following Martin Luther's teaching, of Sola Scriptura and Sola Gracia assert that <u>individuals</u> need mainly to be guided by Holy Scripture and the Holy Spirit

The magisterium is headed by the pope and consists of Bishops from all over the world. A pope is elected, when needed, by a conclave of 120 prominent Cardinals (who had been elevated to that status by a previous pope), and who are still under 80 years old.

Teachings of the magisterium have evolved over time. The idea, held by some outsiders that the Magisterium <u>often</u>* declares their decisions to be infallible (or Dogmatic), is false.

* Declaring something as dogma (called "declaring Ex Cathedra) is very rare. Only two such declarations have been made during the two thousand+ history of the Catholic Church:

1. That Jesus' mother, Mary was born without original sin;

2. That Jesus' mother, Mary, was taken up bodily into heaven.

I think that these two dogmas were made "Ex Cathedra" because they cannot be found out by researching history or by scholarship. This is in contrast to the Magisterim confirming something already widely believed, such as that Jesus is/was both God and man.

Besides a continually working Magisterium, even greater authority is wielded by a Church Ecumenical (or world-wide) Council, also called a Conciliar Magisterium.

Since the first such council, held in Nicaea in 325 AD, in the region which is now Modern Turkey, there have been 21 such councils summoned by various popes.

Pope John. XXIII (declared to be saint in 2014)

In 1958 Pope John XXIII surprised the Catholic world by calling the Second* Vatican Council, to be held in Rome from 1962 to 1965.

*It was called the Second Vatican Council because another council, held just before this one in 1870, also took place in the Vatican.

Over 2000 bishops, thousands of observers, auditors, sisters, laymen and laywomen, from all over the world, came to witness the Second Vatican Council. Theologians (both religious and lay scholars, including non-Catholics), attended and participated in many discussions. But it was only the bishops of the world, and the heads of the main religious orders of men*, called "Council Fathers", who had approved the final documents by their vote. There were thousands such documents, of which maybe the most obvious was the change that Mass could be said in the local vernacular, rather than only in Latin.

Many Catholic nuns subsequently left their vocation. In my opinion, one important reason for this was the apparent disregard of female opinion in using only "the Council <u>Fathers</u>".

This brings me to the controversial issue of birth control, <u>which has not been settled</u> <u>infallibly by the magisterium.</u> It is an issue that bothers me because my biologist training makes me fear overpopulation: Whenever one species of any organism overwhelms the environment, it disrupts ecological balance, and disaster follows.

For example see stories about the Irish potato famine of 1845, which happened because only one species of potato was imported from Peru; or see "Deforestation of the Amazon Rain Forrest" on Wikipedia, which shows that Human expansion has caused the loss of much of this Amazon Rain Forrest, by farming and logging. The Amazon jungle, acting almost like one of the lungs of the world, cleanses the air and regulates climate.

The Catholic Church's opposition to "artificial" birth control is based on the biblical mandate to be fruitful and multiply (Genesis 1:28), advice that was sound in the beginning of time, when the number of people on earth was low, but today overpopulation threatens the balance of nature.

I think the "immigration problem" prominent in today's political scene is a reflection of the overpopulation in "the third world".

On a more personal level I resent encouragement to having <u>large numbers</u> of children by the Catholic Church because it necessarily forces mothers (much more than fathers) to engage exclusively in housework and care of children. (I think this is a reason why mostly men, and only a few women have contributed in major ways to art and science, in the past.)

<u>Originally the Catholic Church seemed to have agreed with my view on birth control:</u>

In 1963, Pope John XXIII called together a commission comprised of fifty-five members, including five married Catholic couples, theologians, priests, and physicians to study the question of whether the church's teaching on artificial contraception should be changed.

To the surprise of conservatives in the church, this commission voted <u>overwhelmingly</u> to recommend that the ban against artificial means of birth control in marriage be lifted. After all, the church accepts the idea of birth control, by the "rhythm method", so why not give couples a more reliable way to limit the number of children. It was felt that having this power would strengthen marriages, as well as society. They declared that responsible parenthood was an essential part of modern marriage and the morality of sexual acts between married couples was not dependent upon the direct fecundify of each, but that every particular act must be viewed within the totality of the marriage.

Pope Paul VI

Despite the commission's work and their theologically unassailable conclusion that the church's teaching on birth control was neither infallible nor irreversible, Pope Paul VI (John XXIII's successor) stunned the world on July 29, 1968, when he reaffirmed the church's ban on modern contraceptives in his encyclical, *Humanae Vitae*. He declared that "each and every marital act must of necessity retain its intrinsic relationship to the procreation of human life." He agreed with a minority report, prepared by four conservative theologian priests on the commission that maintained contraception was a "sin against nature" and a "shameful and intrinsically vicious act."

Since then, despite ecological findings that overabundance of one species leads to disaster, church leaders have coupled their statements against "artificial" birth control with unproven medical reasons for encouraging married couples to produce as many children as is compatible with "the physics [sic], spiritual and mental well-being of the mother and children".

I can't help but wonder, how celibate and male clerics understand what leads to the "mental well-being of the mother and children".

While some church sponsored people have advocated only the "rhythm method" for birth control, most married Catholics have ignored this "official" Catholic position.

To be more than 60% effective the "rhythm method" requires keeping records of the wife's vaginal secretions. It is cumbersome and far from natural, disregarding concern for couples' well-being.

In contrast, barrier methods such as condoms and diaphragms, prevention of ovulation with hormone-containing pills, or by surgically severing the tubes that carry gametes, all prevent fertilization. Therefore, one cannot argue that these methods "kill

God-created souls". (This is the argument made against the use of intrauterine devices that prevent zygote implantation.)

Another church argument against birth control is that manipulating natural biology with hormones may harm the female body. Over decades now, use of hormones, under medical supervision has been shown to be compatible with health, while multiple pregnancies can do harm to the female body, e.g. increased blood pressure, problems with back, abdomen and pelvis.

Despite my disagreement about the church's present thinking on birth control, I see much truth in the Catholic interpretation of Jesus' message of love, and I have confidence that imperfections, creeping into this interpretation from human weaknesses, will be overcome.

My feelings in this context are well summarized in the TV opera "Amahl and the Night Visitors" by Gian Carlo Menotti: One of the Magi kings on their way to see the new-born Jesus says: "On Love He will build His kingdom".

Other books by the Author

She has previously published three novels titled:

"Where is My Home"

"Mind Control"

"Heterosis"

A non-fiction book titled:

"Thoughts on the Origin of Life, and other Essays."

www.ingramcontent.com/pod-product-compliance
Lightning Source LLC
LaVergne TN
LVHW012245070526
838201LV00090B/127